THE HORSES VOICE

BY

ELAINE TYLEY

All rights reserved, no part of this book may be reproduced in whole or in part without written permission from the author Elaine Tyley. Except by reviewers who may quote brief exerts in connection with a review in a newspaper, magazine, or electronic publication; nor may any part of this book be reproduced, stored in a retrieval system, or transmitted in any form or by any means electronic, mechanical, photocopying, recording or other, without written permission from Elaine Tyley.

Copyright © 2014 ELAINE TYLEY

All rights reserved.

ISBN:1495442039
ISBN-13:9781495442032

ACKNOWLEDGMENTS

For Bill who introduced me to the wonderful world of healing, my family for their support and to the horses who have and continue to guide me on my journey to horse.

In memory of Jake my faithful dog and Fee and Grace who taught me so much.

Keep calling and I will come, your voice will be heard.......

HEALING AND THE VETERINARY SURGEONS ACT 1966

Healing - channelling healing energy through the hands from a universal source of energy - should not be used as a substitute for veterinary care and attention.

Please note that Paragraph 18 of Part 2F of the RCVS Guide to Professional Conduct, provides information including that all animals must be seen by a veterinary surgeon, and that the vet must give permission for healing to be given by the laying on of hands.

With any concerns that you may have about an animals' health or wellbeing, your first port of call must be a veterinarian. Only a vet may make a diagnosis, or prescribe.

ALL NAMES OF HORSES, OWNERS AND AREAS HAVE BEEN
CHANGED TO PROTECT IDENTITY

ABOUT THE AUTHOR

Surprisingly, Elaine Tyley was not brought up around horses, she started learning to ride at the age of 12 and had her first horse when she was 21. Elaine has always "heard" horses and thought everyone could, it was a gift she kept to herself until the age of 30 when she hit a wall of depression. A chance meeting with a psychic gave her a message from her Nanny that would change her life. There started a spiritual journey lasting many years, it became a journey, not only back to Elaine but also to horse.

Elaine came out of the closet in 2010 and announced to the world that she could speak horse and from then on Horses Voice has grown. It is now not only Elaine's job but her life, she sees it as her vocation to voice the horses voice. To make people understand, a horse is not born a "problem" but problems arise when mankind starts demanding and not listening......

CONTENTS

1	My Journey	Page 7
2	Lafayette – Fee	Page 25
3	The Bond Between Mother and Foal	Page 31
4	What is Healing?	Page 55
5	The Problem Horse	Page 61
6	Where Have We Gone Wrong?	Page 131
7	Just Because	Page 139
8	The Parting	Page 177
9	The Sales	Page 185
10	The Last Chapter	Page 193

1

MY JOURNEY

"Don't put your hand through the gate," my mother shouted from further up the road, I sighed and put it through anyway. My hand met with the warmth of the dog's hair and his kind eyes looked into mine, we spoke until I was hauled away by Mum telling me I could have been bitten. "He wouldn't bite me" I replied "you don't know that" Mum said "but I do, he was friendly, he spoke to me". "Elaine how many times do I have to tell you dogs' do not talk"………………………………….

But they did and not just dogs' all animals, I could always communicate with them and feel their feelings. There was no barrier it was as simple as talking to Mum. But nobody else seemed to hear the whispers, I could understand my mum's fears she had been bitten as a child and feared all dogs. But for me there was no fear just complete understanding, when I was with the animals I felt complete, at one with them. There were no barriers or confusion with animals that could happen when I was with people; I guess we spoke the same language. My intense love of animals may have seemed strange to some, I was not from a home in the country with loads of animals. I was brought up living in Poole, Dorset a town far away from the place of my dreams. I would Watch Black Beauty, Folly foot and any other horse programs and dream that my life was like the people on the screen, living in the country with horses.

But reality was far from there, I lived in a three bedroom semi detached house in the town; I had my cat Fluffy and the neighbourhood dogs to spend my time with. My parents were not horsey, the only horse contact I had as a child growing up was if we went to a Country Park, a drive in the New Forest or going to find the tethered pony on the common. A local lady used to go to the sales and buy a wild foal; the foal would arrive on the waste ground opposite my house on the end of a chain tethered to the ground. The foal's freedom snatched away from it and all that it had known. I could feel the foals sadness and pain. This would then manifest itself into anger as the foal galloped round and round trying to pull the chain from the ground and be able to move as it once had. I would spend hours sitting out there sending comfort and giving the foal carrots and water, hoping that in some way I was providing the foal comfort. Some days the foal would be so sad and other days filled with rage at having its freedom taken away. The foal would be moved to the common when it had run out of grass and off I would go with the neighbourhood dogs clutching my bag of carefully chopped carrots. Until the day came when I could not find the foal, I would look everywhere until I realised that the foal had been sold on and I would never see it again. I would feel intense sadness and at the same time send my love out to the foal hoping that she had been found a good home.

It is hard to describe my communication with animals, the only way I can explain it is that from a young age I had a loss of hearing and this was not discovered until I was 12 years old. So for a long time, I did not hear as others did. I heard well enough to have normal speech but I believe having the deafness gave me the gift of being able to communicate on another level. On a frequency that is the same as animals, I had absolutely no fear of animals as a child because they told me they would not hurt me. For me, being with the animals was more natural than with people. When I was given my first hearing aids I wore them out of Poole hospital and I could not believe how noisy the world was. The traffic, people's voices, were to me so overpowering, as we went back to the car we walked through Poole Park. It was then that I realised I had never heard the birds' song before, that feeling of hearing their voices for the first time will never leave me. So the aids brought me the sounds of nature but they also brought me the noise of everyday life, it was too much and I decided not to wear them. I stayed in my quiet world then at about the same time my dreams came true.

A family friend Clare told me about the riding lessons she was having. We decided it would be great if I could go with her and I set about persuading my parents. At last they agreed and I joined Clare one Saturday and caught the mini bus to the riding stables in Christchurch. I was only allowed to go every other week but this became the highlight of my life.   To at last be in a horsey place to feel their warmth under my hand and smell their own unique smell. I learnt to ride in a very basic manner on the selection of ponies that they had, fell off a few times to but it was never enough to put me off. Before we caught the bus home the ponies would be put out in the field and the owner of the yard let everyone ride them out bareback and race them up and down the field. I was never happy seeing this as the ponies had worked hard all day. Clare and I were always given the old lady to ride out, but we didn't join in with the race, one of us would sit on her back while the other led her out and then we would stand and let her graze until the others had finished. The other children could not understand why we were not racing her, but that poor old girl was tired and I could feel the ache in her bones. To stand and stroke her as she grazed and give her my love was far more important to me.

I carried on learning to ride and changed stables to where they had a school and had "proper" lessons, but I never seemed to do very well as I would not kick them or pull on the reins. All I wanted to give them was love and understanding, it was soon agreed that I was far better going for a hack where I could ride out, talking to my horse and in a complete world of my own. I carried on being allowed to ride twice a month and every year I would enter the "win a pony" competition hoping that I would win the Palomino pony but I never did.   I can remember on my 13th Birthday my treat was to go for a two hour ride out in the New Forest. As my birthday is in January the day was cold with a sharp frost and the Forest was white, I arrived at the stables so excited.

The Forest was like the place of my dreams it was horsey heaven it was where they could roam free, an illusion that was shattered as you will read later on. To ride on the Forest was the best present ever, I can still remember it as if it was yesterday, the sights the smells. More importantly it was the longest ride I had ever had two hours of sheer bliss.

My animal communication I suppose I took for granted, as a child I never really thought about it, it was as natural as talking to people. I thought everyone could hear them, it was only when I was seventeen and out during a break from work with a colleague that I realised nobody else heard them. I had stopped and spoke to a dog tied up outside the shop. I could feel from him that he was scared and he was desperately looking for his Mum but he could not see her through the sea of feet and legs. I put out my hand and stroked his head and then got down on his level and asked him how he was and told him his mum would be back soon. I stood up to find my work colleague staring at me and looking concerned "do you always do that" she asked. I asked her what she meant, "that talking to the dog" "well yes I replied don't you?" she looked at me and replied "no" and walked away.

I looked around me and saw all the people perhaps for the first time and I have to say that nobody else really noticed the dog. In fact none of them really noticed anything, all they were focused on was moving forward into the shop or leaving it. It was then that I realised that perhaps I was a bit different; perhaps this was the reason why I found it hard to make friends as a child and spent my time with the dogs. I went back into work thinking about this, at the time I wanted to be accepted as normal and be asked to parties, so I made a decision. For years I had not worn my hearing aids on a regular basis and by doing this I missed out on a lot of conversation and I guess people got fed up with me. When you can't hear you tend to smile in what you think are the right places, when really you don't have a clue what is being said. I realised that day that if I wanted to be truly accepted and be invited out to parties I needed to hear. So I turned the hearing aids on to the noisy world and turned the voices off and went off and had a good time being "normal".

I still rode whenever I could afford to and then at the age of 21 I moved to the country and I was able to buy my first horse Red. Red was a 16hh chestnut Thoroughbred x Irish Draft when I had him vetted it was found that he had a serious heart murmur. Although the vets had given me this information I carried on and brought him, I didn't feel that it caused him any problems. Red taught me a lot about owning a horse and I was very lucky to keep him at a private yard where I learnt an awful lot. We didn't compete or take life to serious, we would do sponsored rides and enjoyed hacking around the countryside. Red was my dream come true, my very own horse. Red became a part of my learning horse, there is only so much you can learn from riding schools. I can remember him arriving and as well as my immense joy there was also an element of fear. Would I be able to cope? did I know enough? The questions were endless, but Red took me under his wing and taught me horse, he could be challenging would some times take off across a field with me holding on for dear life, but he never tried to get rid of me, what ever he did he took me with him, even if it wasn't all my own choice! I had a wonderful six years with Red the heart murmur caused him know problems but unfortunately at the age of 19 colic did and I had to have him put to sleep. I give thanks now to Red as he was a huge part of my journey of learning "horse" and also a dream come true.

Life carried on and I married, separated and divorced, then after a couple of years I met Richard who I married and had 2 children Laura and James. Richard was a dairy farmer and in time we also set up a successful livery yard. So during this period of my life I felt life was good I was surrounded by animals and I could also help others who crossed my path. I loved having the yard and spent most of my time there making sure all the horses were relaxed and happy. As time went on I found living on the farm hard, I loved the new born calves that I looked after but I hated the life that they would lead later on. I was at war with who I really was, the animal communicator who could hear their calls and the Farmer's wife.

It all became too much, it was at the time of the BSE crisis, with the worry of our own cows being infected and seeing the news and the way the animals were being killed and burnt tore me apart. It was also at this time that my uncle died, I had not been close to him but after his funeral I fell apart and a black cloud of depression hit me.

During this dark period in my life I had counseling and during one session I was taken back to find my inner-child. I had to give her a name and I called her Junior, the counselor asked me about Junior and who she was with. I told her she was with my cat Fluffy and then all of a sudden out of the blue I looked at my counselor and told her she was going to think I was mad. She encouraged me to carry on talking and I told her "I can speak to animals", I don't know how I do it but it is something that I have done all my life. It was like a light bulb moment as if a huge curtain had been pulled back from which I had been hiding behind. Everything came flooding back to me, how, when I was 16 I went to find Fluffy before I went to work and he told me he would not be there when I returned. I went off to work worried and sure enough I came home to find that during the day he had suffered a stroke and had died. I told her about the tethered pony I used to spend my time with and the dogs. I realised by shutting down the communication I had shut off a huge part of me that needed to be reopened.

My life had been on the wrong path for years, I had spent so long trying to please others that I had totally ignored who I really am. Turning my back on the animals, I had also turned my back on myself and I was only half the person I should be. By trying to become "normal" I had shut myself down from feeling what I truly felt. Things always never seemed quite right, as if I was missing something and it was during this session that the curtain was pulled back and I understood my depression was because I was on the wrong path, but quite what the right path was I had no idea. But I didn't have long to wait to find out.

I was beginning to feel better when one morning I picked up the local paper and an advert caught my eye. 'Psychic Evening 'I had never been to anything like this before but I knew I had to go, it was being held in the next village so I asked a friend to join me and off we went.

The evening was being run by the late Bill Harrison, as I took my seat I picked him out easily enough by his loud waistcoat and wonderful smile and laugh. The evening began pretty much as you see on television, you are given a microphone and a message is passed to you from those passed over. I found the whole thing very interesting and all of a sudden the microphone was placed in my hand and Bill said "I have a message for you from your Nan". I confirmed that Nanny had passed over and felt the hairs on the back of my neck stand up.

Bill went onto describe Nanny from her lovely smile, her short height and the twin sets she used to wear. But what totally convinced me was when he described her hearing aid which was the box pinned to her jumper and a wire going up to her ear-piece and also her Salvation Army uniform. Nanny wore her uniform with pride, she wore the bonnet with the big bow under her chin and the army was her life. Bill went onto tell me that I had inherited not only my Nanny's deafness but also her healing hands.   He then said "you talk to animals don't you" I confirmed that this is something I have always done. "With your speaking to the animals and healing you can really help the horse which is what you should be doing. Come and see me after and we will have a chat".

To say I was blown away was an understatement, but I stayed until the end and went and had a chat with Bill, which is possibly the best thing I have ever done. He told me that everything I had was natural, he wanted to know why I didn't tell people about the communication. I explained that when you have been doing it all your life you think everyone can do it, it was only when I was told that I was strange that I started to hide my gift. He told me it was now time to stop hiding and to start healing.

After my chance meeting with Bill I arranged to go and see him at his healing sanctuary and there started years of advice, training and mentoring until his death. I sometimes went months without seeing Bill but he was always there when I needed advice and that was very important. He used to say to me "get on with it, there is nothing that anyone can teach you, the ability you have is a gift."

The spiritual healing was totally alien to me, I was not really religious, I had gone to the Salvation Army as a child and church with the school and that was all. Thinking about what Bill had said about Nanny I realised that her healing gift was with people, I used to go and visit and there would always be people sat in the arm chair discussing their problems with Nanny. She seemed to unravel the confusion for them and they would leave with a better understanding of their problem and a clearer picture of the way ahead. After talking to Bill I realised that the spirits were there to guide me on my journey of finding out who I am, destination unknown.

I didn't tell many people about my healing ability I knew lots of people would find it strange and suspicious that I suddenly had these powers! I started reading and studying everything I could find on healing so that I had a chance of understanding exactly what I was supposed to be doing! At this time there were not many books on healing horses so I studied healing in general. I looked at Reiki which then was very popular and acceptable and I felt perhaps this was my path. I phoned Bill and he said I did not need Reiki and that I just needed "to get on with it."

I didn't take Bill's advice! I had a friend who was a Reiki master and she said that she would attune me as a present. I went to her house and the proceedings started and after the meditation she asked me to put my hands above my head so they were shoulder width apart. The attunement then started and I had to bring my hands together. But I couldn't It was like I had a brick wall between my hands and there was no way in this world that they would come together. Anna my friend stopped and I apologised and told her that I could not do it, something was stopping me being attuned to Reiki. I later phoned Bill and told him about the experience and his reply was "I told you, you do not need Reiki what you have is pure, stronger than anything that you could be attuned to." I thought about this for a while and then decided that perhaps I would listen to Bill and "get on with it" so I did just that I started healing a horse which belonged to Liz a friend of mine and she then introduced me to a wonderful lady who became a good friend called Sarah who let me use her yard for my case studies. During this time I also donated a raffle prize to a charity for a horse healing, a lady in Weymouth won it and I was booked to treat her horse.

I went feeling slightly nervous, I knocked at the door and the lady told me that the horse was in the stable and to knock the door when I had finished. Obviously there was not much interest in my work from his owner so off I went to find Sam. Sure enough he was in his stable and I introduced myself over the door and put his head collar on, when I entered the stable Sam came across as a very calm horse and quite happy to accept healing from me.

I felt over his body and located areas of heat where he was holding onto old negative energy and I started healing the areas down through his back. As I was healing I asked Sam if there was anything troubling him. His eyes became heavy and he started licking and chewing as he released the negative energy in his body. Then I was drawn to his sheath area and Sam showed me images of his penis it was very sore and the whole area was swollen. I focused on healing this area to release the memory and blocked energy from this experience and he relaxed and yawned and when he was comfortable I finished the healing.

I argued with myself as I walked back to his owner whether to mention the details given to me about his sheath area but felt uncomfortable with it and perhaps thought I had imagined it and it couldn't be true. I knocked the door and told his owner that her horse had enjoyed the healing and there didn't seem to be any major issues past or present. Sam's owner replied "Oh if you had told me about the infection he had two years ago around his sheath and penis I would have believed you were good! Thanks for seeing him" and closed the door. I walked down the drive kicking myself.

Shortly after this Sarah had given my phone number to one of her pupils as her horse kept on going lame and the vet and the physio could not find out what was wrong. After treating Sam my confidence had taken a bit of a battering and I agreed with myself that I would say everything that the horse told me. I arrived at the yard and Shelia came out to meet me and took me to see her horse "Rose". Shelia explained that the lameness had been going on for months and nobody seemed to know what was causing it.

As I walked into Rose's stable she told me straight away that she had "sore feet". I felt her hooves and I felt an area of heat in both front hooves. I told Shelia what Rose had said to me and that she should ask her vet to x-ray the hooves. I carried on healing Rose who relaxed and was very grateful that someone had listened to her. The following week Rose's hooves were x-rayed and it was found that her pedal bones had rotated and the pressure and pain was making Rose lame. The farrier was brought in and with corrective shoeing Rose has continued to have a lovely hacking life, I still see her out and about today. As you can imagine Rose really boosted my confidence, but I still had so many questions and I decided that if I was to be of any use to the horses I needed to study. There started twelve years of studying; I could not afford courses so I studied at home, everything I could find on healing, horses, and communication.

I also studied myself and who I am, not who I had become but the real me the person I should have been all along. I took apart my communication ability, my healing hands; I studied healing, the universe, spirit and Mother Nature. I then took apart horse behavior and how horses communicate and found out just why horses did what they did. I looked at their survival in wild herds and how humans have affected these beautiful animals and over time turned them into robots to boost our ego.

I studied both human and horse and opened myself to spirit; I learnt how connection with our spirit guides can bring confidence and understanding into our lives. Finally, I understood exactly who I was and what I could do. Then after 12 years of relentless studying fueling my hunger and passion I decided it was time to go back to everything that I had taken apart. Pick up my communication and healing and put it back together to become who I am now "The Horses Voice".

Through my healing therapy I can explain why horses do what they do, what has caused it, heal the area and help the owner to understand their horse so that their relationship can flourish. Some have called me the horse counselor and to some degree that is what I do. People ask me to explain exactly what I do to horses. It is a question I am not very good at answering, I am an animal communicator it is not something I have trained to do but simply what I have always done. My ability to communicate with horses is often better than with people.

During my years of studying I healed many horses but still felt that something was missing, I didn't want to just heal I wanted to provide a completely different approach and for this I let the horses guide me. I studied all forms of Natural Horsemanship and asked the horses what they thought. I went to competitions and listened to their opinions, I went to a hunt meet to stand and listen, x-country, dressage, all the events that we take horses to.

The results were amazing, the whispers and screams were heart breaking and I promised that in some way I would try and make people listen. Some people think I am a fruit cake but slowly things are changing for the horses and I. During the summer of 2012 I took the step of handing in my notice giving up my cleaning jobs and giving myself to the horses, from then on Spirit became a very big addition to my life. They have joined forces with me and guide me on everything that I do. So what do I call myself? I am a spiritual healer but this title sometimes scares people, I work with energy within the body, slightly more acceptable. But what it has become is a counseling service, sometimes for both horse and rider. I write up some of my visits for people to read on my website and facebook page, people email to say they enjoy my stories. But unfortunately they are not stories, they are case notes about horses feelings as real and raw as yours or mine but, they belong to the horse.

So you see everything you read in this book is as real as a person revealing their inner most turmoil, some funny, a lot distressing and many sad, all of this is revealed during the therapy session. I start all therapy sessions by talking to the horse and asking if they would like my help. I then carry on communicating with the horse and locating in their body where the emotions are held from past trauma. I then explain to the horses owner exactly where the horse is stiff, which would be the better rein, I tell them the character and personality of their horse and then dowse over the horses body so that they can see the reaction of the pendulum over the blocked areas.

I then start to heal the area; it is like a rose with layers of petals. The first layer is the block in the body, you heal the block which is there for protection, it enables the horse to put up a barrier to stop the pain, their owners see this barrier as a bite, kick, anger, miserable etc. to me it is the barrier to the emotion.

Then I peel back the layer revealing the emotion behind the block, revealing the raw emotion and the next layer the cause. Sometimes this could take a few sessions, during the whole time the horse is Licking and chewing and yawning releasing the block to the universe. Sometimes they will be reliving the fight, anger and frustration with me and I may be pulled around, knocked into walls, bitten or they may even try to kick out as the anger is released. At the end of the session the horse can be exhausted it takes a lot of energy to release the emotions but by doing so the horse can relax in every way. Mind, body, muscles and some even lie down and fall into a big sleep.

By releasing the energy blocks and counseling them through the event that has caused it I bring them peace. The owners see the difference and they feel the difference not only on the ground but also when they ride. The stiffness has gone, the body and mind is relaxed and the owner understands their horse and begins to work with the horse and their relationship will never be the same again. The session opens their eyes to who their horse is, not an animal to be dominated and abused but a being that feels more than you can ever imagine. The emotions that are released during the session also forces the owner to break the emotional barrier and release their anxieties as well.

So you see, my journey has barely started, as I said earlier destination unknown. I guess I should describe myself as the horse counselor for mind, body and spirit because when they are allowed to speak, their world becomes a better place.

As you read this book, I ask you to think about your horse, what is your horse communicating to you. Remember, communication can come as a kick, bite, walking away from you, bucking, rearing, the list is endless. But it is the only way they can make themselves heard and if you don't listen the communication from them will become stronger and stronger…..

2

LAFAYETTE - FEE

There have been many horses that I met during my years when I was training and since, who I will tell you about. They were very important to me as they were teaching and guiding me and making me aware of what I could do and how the horses needed me to help them. One very important horse that came into my life during this time was a mare called Lafayette (Fee)

Fee came into my life through a very special friend. I was in a bad place, recently had depression and I had had a bad fall from a young horse resulting in the mare not being ridden again due to back injury. I was about ready to give up on everything. At this time a friend of mine Julie persuaded me to visit a lady called Sarah who had a dressage yard and was interested in her horses being used as case studies. I explained to Julie that I did not feel in the best place for healing but was persuaded to go up and meet Sarah and her horses. As a result of this meeting I made a very special friend in Sarah who has supported me along with Julie, they both encouraged me to forge ahead with my work.

I arranged to go to Sarah's yard to start my case studies, I did not take payment for the case studies and after treating one of Sarah's horses she offered me a lesson on her advanced dressage horse Fee. At first I declined, I was not a dressage rider and since the accident my confidence was at rock bottom. However, over time I was persuaded to put my foot in the stirrup again. Sarah was aware of how I was feeling and told me that I could just walk around the school. I mounted Fee and was very confused to find she was in a double bridle! I had never ridden in a double bridle before so after this had been explained to me and when I was happy we entered the arena.

Even at walk the feeling of Fee was incredible, she had so much presence and power and at the same time stability. It almost felt like Fee had put a safety blanket around me and made me feel safe. We walked around the school with Sarah walking beside us until I felt happy and then I asked for a trot. By the end of the forty five minutes I had not only trotted and cantered but with Sarah's instruction Fee had taken me through flying changes! Which I was later to realise was her party piece, I felt ten foot tall after the lesson and so much better in myself and my life. Fee in that lesson made me realise that I did have lots to offer and I could ride again.

The following day I received a phone call from Sarah making me an offer. Fee's owner had decided that at eighteen Fee needed to retire from serious competing and they wanted to know if I would like to have her. I was totally shocked and told Sarah that I wasn't a good enough rider, she told me to think about it. A few hours later, after I had got over the shock I phoned Sarah and said "I would love to have Fee" and she joined me at my yard the following week.

Fee arrived, I had been told that she did not like to go out for long and that after twenty minutes she would need to go into her stable. When I had healed Fee before I always felt that she had part of herself locked away, she was going through the motions but her spirit was not as bright as it could have been. So when Fee arrived I turned her out and told her that she could come back in if she wished or she could start being a horse again. After twenty minutes I went back to the field and Fee was happy grazing with her new friends, so I left her out and within a week she was out twenty four hours a day learning to be a horse again.

Fee had had a hard start in life she was bred in Germany and had received some hard handling; she had come back with a hard attitude, mirroring her trainers. She had been put into a double bridle at the age of three and taught the "German way". Fee had done a lot of travelling in her life due to her owner being in the forces and I felt that she now realised that she had her forever home. Sarah was keen for me to learn from Fee as she was an amazing school mistress, but Sarah despaired of me. During our lesson Sarah would give me instructions, Fee would communicate with me and I would burst out laughing as Fee told me what she thought of that and we would do something entirely different!.

During this time I was communicating with and healing Fee and my other horses but I was not being true to myself and was being led by my ego to fit in with the horsey set. I was very different to the person I am now, I carried on doing low level dressage with Fee until at twenty Fee told me she had had enough and so our life settled down to hacking around the beautiful Somerset lanes. Fee thoroughly enjoyed this time in her life, she was often very naughty and if she decided to stop the traffic she did in spectacular fashion!

The years carried on and Fee taught me how to live again, as she became older and her body started to ache I told her to tell me when she no longer wanted to be ridden. Sure enough the day came when I approached her stable with the tack and she turned and walked to the back of her box. I put the tack down and went to her and told her it was ok and I never rode her again. This was a very sad time for me but I had always told Fee that her ridden life had been hard and it would be her choice when she stopped being ridden. Fee had taught me to have confidence in myself and that I could ride and feel free again, instead of constantly worrying she taught me to live.

Fee then retired to the field and kept an eye on the other horses on the yard; she was definitely in charge and whatever she said the others did.

Fee had taught me an awful lot at a very important time of my life, a time when I was discovering who I was not the person expected from my parents or friends but who I was deep inside. I was the lady who could talk to horses and my journey was well on its way.

3

THE BOND BETWEEN MOTHER AND FOAL

One of the biggest issues I come across that causes lasting damage to the horse is the weaning process. More often than not the mares keep the foal with them until they are about 6 months old and then they are weaned, unfortunately for some this is done even younger. A lot of people simply take the mare or foal and remove them to another yard, or the foal is taken and locked in a stable both doors closed to stop it coming over the door. The screams from both mother and foal can be heard for miles around.

One of my biggest arguments with mankind is that horses feel the same emotions as us, imagine what would happen if at 6 months old a child is removed from its mother, no warning, no time to say goodbye. The feelings felt by the human mother would be dreadful, heart breaking, yet mankind believes it to be acceptable to do the same to a horse, who, I know feels the same as any woman. Perhaps the following will make you think;

GRACE

Grace is my horse, I found her in 2004 at a dealers in Somerset. When I first saw her I looked into the saddest most haunted eye that I have ever seen.

Grace was incredibly stressed in her stable, box walking and not at all happy, I suggested we bring her out into the yard so that I could see her properly. I felt her over and her body was a mass of damaged energy, deep rooted emotions that needed to be voiced. Her eyes were a mirror to her soul and it was so deep and haunted the emotional disturbance within was huge. She was very poor, you could see her ribs, her pelvis was all bone and there was no muscle on her body. I knew I had to help her and struck a deal with the dealer and came home to get my trailer and went back to collect her. I was told that she would travel fine she had after all come over from Belgium, but he did advise me to "drive as soon as she is loaded"

Once safely in the box I drove Grace away with her screams for her friends ringing in my ears. By the time I got home she was covered in sweat and her eyes had taken on a vacant haunted expression. She had no idea who I was or where she was, it was just another destination on her road through hell which was her life. I decided to turn her out with Fee in the hope that she would relax, Fee watched from a distance as Grace galloped around the field screaming for her friends who could no longer hear her. As the gallop became a canter and then a trot Grace's screams became less frequent until she stood and looked out of those haunted eyes at this new destination. She lowered her head and Fee walked towards her licking and chewing and offering friendship, they started to graze side by side.

Later on that day I caught them both and brought them into the barn and introduced Grace to her stable, she was not at all happy shut inside and the feeling of panic and separation was huge. I realised that Grace's separation anxiety was the worst I had ever seen, she could not be on her own, it was more than she could cope with, I decided to arrange the stables so that Fee was opposite and she settled for a little while to eat her hay. Every noise or movement would alert Grace to possible danger, she was on high alert the flight mode was never far away. With that complete panic about being shut in, feeling insecure and the risk of being left on her own there was no way she could relax.

It soon became apparent that Grace could not cope with any horses in the yard leaving the stable block, my mornings started very early so that I could get Grace out with Fee before any other horse was moved. I kept her out as much as possible, only bringing them in when the weather and ground dictated. I spent a long time out in the field with Grace watching her every move, I would sit there and watch her anxiety, high alert always there. The fence became her zone out friend she would pace up and down with the eye switched off, in her own place I would call hell. I would call her to try and get her attention but there was nobody home. This was painful enough to watch but there was another gear to Grace's stress, if she was panicked by anything she would gallop the fence line until she was white with sweat, then her eyes would be big and staring and the fear within was immense.

I realised that all of what I had studied over the years would come into use, at the time I wasn't sure in what way but I knew I was about to take a journey with Grace. It became a journey of finding Grace and giving her peace. We needed to talk about her past; the foals which had been so brutally taken, the beatings from the men and through it all I had to seek her forgiveness. After all I am human the same species as those who have tortured her soul.

I started healing Grace out in the field, at first she would only take the healing for a short while; to relax too much she thought would put her in danger. When you are relaxed you cannot be on high alert, ready to flee at any time. Can you imagine how mentally exhausted Grace was, to be on alert twenty four hours a day not trusting anyone or anything. As she started to trust me the healings became a little longer until one day she let out a huge sigh lowered her head and let me in. She opened her heart to me, the heart where all the intense sadness and grief was held. The intense emotion that came over me I will never forget, it was like throwing a stone in to a lake and the ripples go on forever. Her eye was so sad all I had to do was look at her and I cried her tears.

During the healing sessions I could see her foal being taken and how hard she fought to keep her, but the men were to strong and they took the foal away. I could see her standing staring through a hole in the barn wall watching and screaming unable to rescue her baby. The screams continued until there was silence and the foal could not be heard anymore. There are no words to describe the heart break that Grace felt as her baby was taken. Many of you will have met Grace she is the most loving horse I have ever come across and the pain was intense and broke her heart.

As Grace started to accept her stable sometimes she would stand and watch through a hole in her stable wall. There was nothing to see and it was after this healing that I realised that little hole in the wall reminded her of the times her foals were taken. She stood there in the hope that one day she would see one of her foals return. I used crystals in her stable to help with the healing process; rose quartz was dotted around on the beams to help with her emotional stress.

It wasn't long before I realised that I needed the help of another healer as I was too emotionally involved with Grace to help her. I called out a local healer who took one look at Grace's eye and the emotion and sadness hit her. I told Jill what I knew of Grace, she had been a brood mare in Belgium and then brought over to the UK. She had gone to the auction but was so poor nobody brought her so ended up at the dealer's yard. The vet thought she was about 12 and had confirmed that her body was sound but her mind was another thing! Jill picked up on the grief that Grace felt, it was the grief from losing her babies, having them taken, she had put up a fight but the men had won. She saw as I did, the separation and she picked up on the heaviness of Graces heart brought about by the huge emotional experience of the foals being taken. Imagine how you would feel if your six month old baby was one day taken never to be seen again, imagine the fight you would fight for your baby, only to be beaten down and watch your baby being carried away screaming for you and you for them. This is exactly what Grace had been through but not only once she had shown me four foals, four times she grieved for her babies imagine if this was you, how would you feel.

Jill carried out a healing on Grace's heart and as she put it "to let the tar out" the emotional grief was being held in Grace's heart and needed to be released so that she could begin to heal emotionally. As she did this Grace's eyes became heavy, she licked and chewed and relaxed 100% which would have been the first time she had done this for a long time.

Grace's grief and sadness was the same that any lady would feel having her baby taken from her never to see it again. People have to start realising that the way the foals are weaned has a huge effect on the mare who after all is the mother. She has carried the foal for eleven months, felt it move inside and given birth, fed and given unconditional love for six months as any mother does.

Grace became more relaxed after the healing with Jill and I felt that the huge wave of grief was subsiding; I carried on healing her and spending time out in the field building a relationship with her. I would sit and read in the field and Grace would be near by grazing and happy in my company. She still had huge separation anxiety and I knew that this was something that would be with us for the rest of Grace's life. During one healing Grace showed me more details of when one of her foals had been taken she was in a barn, the bedding was soiled and there were a group of mares and foals together. Everything was quiet and peaceful when all of a sudden there were voices, men talking, she could hear lots of activity outside the barn. The door opened and the men came in one of them held on to Grace and the other grabbing her foal and pushing it outside. Grace was full of panic and did all that she could to get away from the man, her instinct was to protect her foal and this energy holding her was stopping her. She put up an enormous fight screaming and pushing but the foal was pushed out of the door and the door shut. Grace was in turmoil, she paced the walls calling and calling, she could hear her foal but could not get to it. Then there was movement behind the barn and through a hole in the wood Grace watched her foal being taken away she was calling and calling and the foal called back, until there was silence. Grace stood looking through that hole for hours with every minute her heart became heavier the sadness overwhelming. As I was shown the pictures I felt her grief and let the tears fall, there are no words to describe how I felt at this moment, Grace yawned and yawned as the anxiety was released and her story told.

Through every healing Grace showed me more and more of her life and what had made her become the stressed horse that she now was. Once Grace started to feel more settled I started taking her into the school to play with her on the ground. During my years of studying the horse I had watched the exchange of energy between horses in the herd and how they communicated with each other and I needed to use this with Grace. Too many horses are expected to understand human talk; if we could learn the energy communication of horse then we have a way of calming and communicating with them. Grace's first reaction to anything new was fear, straight into flight mode, I needed to reach her and engage the thinking side of her brain before the flight took over. I started with her being on a head collar and introduced my form of energy communication to her which she soon understood. I had Grace on a long rope and worked her body in different directions so that she had to think about what I was asking; if she was thinking there was nothing to fear. Thinking kept her attention on me and out of flight and panic mode, these sessions were kept short as it made her very tired. Thinking can be quite exhausting to a horse especially when they have survived in flight mode for such a long time.

After a while I introduced the saddle and bridle to her, the dealer said that he had backed her, but I started as if nothing had been done before. Grace accepted the saddle and bridle; we carried on with the ground work until I decided to ask Grace if she would stand by the mounting box that I had brought into the arena. Straight away the thinking process left her body and the box was obviously the biggest monster she had ever seen. So I brought the box to her and let her sniff it and then I let it touch her body so that she realised it was nothing to fear, I again spoke to her and asked her to stand by the box which she did, I thanked her and took her to her field to turn her out with her friend.

Everything that I did with Grace had to be done in short sessions, with one intention, to stand by the mounting block was the intention of the day. Then lots of praise and she could go back out to her friends. This was something else I had learnt from Grace in the early days, although she had huge separation anxiety it was ok to take her from her friend but not her friend from her. In her mind she had the choice of going back and knew that she would. If her friends were taken from her she panicked thinking that they would never return, like her foals.

The next time in the school I asked Grace if I could put my foot in the stirrup, again she was not too sure about this so we stood at the mounting box and thought about it for a moment, eventually when she was ready I put my foot in the stirrup and bounced a couple of times. Grace accepted this and I thanked her and took her back to her friend in the field. We went through the whole process of mounting like this, it took a long while, some days the flight mode and panic kicked in so we went back a few steps until she was happy and feeling secure again.

The day I did get on her properly was amazing she stood quietly for me to mount, when both feet were in the stirrups I gave her a mint and got off. People watching, I know, thought I was mad, but if I was to have a good relationship with Grace It had to de done at a speed where she stayed calm.

Over a period of time I was able to ride Grace, not as others would ride her, but by using my Communication and my energy we were able to work out a system that worked for us. At that time I had a lesson but it soon became obvious that Grace could not cope with the pressure and I decided that all I needed from Grace was to be able to be with her and go for hacks.

On one such hack we came across a car and trailer filled with plastic parked by the side of the road. Grace went into flight mode straight away and tried to run back up the road. I stopped her and the lady with the trailer asked if she could help in anyway. I asked her to sit on the corner of the trailer which she did and I asked Grace to walk past it which to the ladies amazement she did "what was the difference?" she asked, "now it's a seat and not a monster trailer" I replied. You see if you understand the way your horse thinks life can become so much easier!

Grace and I now have a fantastic time, out hacking on the Dorset hills, never on our own but with her friend. It doesn't take much to change her, if the hunt or shoot come near then the flight and panic mode kick in and she becomes very stressed, but I can soon calm her and bring her energy back down. We now have a small herd of six horses and ponies and she sees herself as the mother of them all. This can be exhausting for her because she is on alert at all times. If the others are sleeping she will always be the one stood up on guard. They are all brought in on a regular basis so that she knows everyone is safe and then she sleeps.

People have often said to me that it was just as well I went to see her on that day because nobody else would have coped with her or understood her. I am pleased I did, Grace and I are on a journey together and I am glad that I have managed to repair some of the damage created by man on this beautiful mare whose only crime was to be a loving mother.

I am called out to treat many horses who have been scarred by the weaning process, for some it can bring about labels such as "problem horse". But the only problem has been the insensitivity of mankind which scars the mare for life and also the foals for they suffer as well. Years ago I witnessed a weaning, a lady I knew had a saddle for sale which I went to look at; whilst I was there she left me as there was a commotion in the yard. She ran out and I followed to see what was happening. As I turned the corner I witnessed a foal being forced into a stable and then both doors being bolted. The stable would have been dark and a frightening place. The foal was screaming, the mare was screaming back as the trailer they had put her in was driven away. I couldn't believe what I was seeing and asked them why they had done this. "Oh to wean the foal, she is five months old and they have to be separated". I asked them what they would now do with the foal, her reply horrified me. The foal was to be kept in the shut stable with water and hay being put in every day, there was to be no attention or bonding, just left. The last time I saw the foal she was stood shaking and in shock in the corner of the stable.

Why? Why do this? The only answer is for money, the mare was going off to the stud and the foal was going up for sale. Have we as human beings become so removed from feeling and emotions in the quest for greed, that we no longer care? We have a lot to learn.

CLEO

I was called out by a lady called Lisa who was very stressed and through that emotion I could feel terror, Lisa was scared. She told me that she had brought a mare called Cleo from a dealer and she needed help to understand what was going on with her. Cleo was becoming more and more difficult to control, Lisa could feel that there was something going on but she did not know how to help Cleo.

I arrived at the address to meet Lisa and Cleo who is a shire x so a big girl in size and strength. Cleo was also a very stressed mare, her eyes were haunted and on alert at all times. Her coat was dull and her whole body was rigid everything was held on full alert and waiting to explode. Lisa was not an experienced horse woman with years of experience, but when she saw Cleo at a dealer's yard she knew that she had to buy her, the horse needed her and perhaps she needed Cleo. Lisa is very holistic and had been trying to reach Cleo, she had got so far but then hit a brick wall; no two days were the same. Lisa was very stressed and had become a little afraid of Cleo, they were going around in circles. It is very difficult when dealing with horses not to feel their pain and anguish and Lisa was definitely feeling Cleo's. They were both mirroring each other, as Lisa drove to the yard she was thinking about how Cleo would be and this made her nervous, Cleo is a big girl and when she decides to blow she blows. When Lisa approached Cleo's stable she would already be nervous and this is the energy that Cleo read and it made her nervous, the more nervous each of them became the more anxious they both were.

I felt Cleo over, the tension within her body was immense, I felt huge heat around her pelvis which she was not at all happy about me touching. So I started on her shoulder and slowly worked my way down her body, as soon as I got near her back end she became very agitated and swung her bottom towards me shaking her head and becoming very cross. I could feel that this was where Cleo stored all her anxiety and emotion, it felt like a volcano which was about to erupt. I stayed working on the area, flashing images came into my mind, big men holding her, using all their strength against her as Cleo's foal was being taken. She was showing me pictures of the weaning and it was heart breaking,

Cleo was fighting with all she could to protect her foal from the men, but they used a lot of force, they came up to her with metal gates, forcing her back behind the gates and grabbed the foal. Cleo was going mad and fought and fought but she was driven back to the corner of the barn and her foal was taken. The screams coming from deep within Cleo were matched by the screams of her foal until there were no more sounds and Cleo was in the barn distraught heartbroken and grieving. During this Cleo and I were circling the box she was in a frenzy of emotions, intense anger, sadness, loneliness, fear and more, all stored within her body. As we went round the box I was sending healing through to her, I felt every emotion and the tears fell from my eyes until Cleo was spent.

Her eyes became soft and her energy lowered, she licked and chewed and sighed, as she yawned and yawned I kept my hand on her heart and she looked at me, really looked at me from deep within her soul. Cleo had been deeply hurt and the pain had gone deep, to lose her foal in such a brutal way was more than she could bear and the pain had been buried deep inside. To see a person who could help her through this pain was a new experience for Cleo, as she looked at me we truly connected, me sending her love and understanding and her thanking me. As a result of the healing Cleo's body needed to adjust, she was at last relaxed and it would take time for her muscles to adjust. Like us when you are full of stress and anger you will have bad shoulders, back, neck, pelvis where ever you hold tension and horses are the same. When we deal with the emotion and release it our muscles relax, you will feel your shoulders drop. You will then be left with soreness as everything rebalances.

As a result of the way Cleo's foal was taken Cleo had become very angry and also possessive over other horses, she feared change, although she was now in a lovely home she feared the fact that it could change and she needed to learn how to trust again. Because of her insecurities she was almost giving Lisa enough ammunition to make the change happen, so if you like she could be proved right. In that way she still held onto control even if it brought the wrong outcome, control is what Cleo understood and gave her power. This is why Cleo had been through many owners and ended up at the dealer's yard.

Lisa was quite shocked about how deep Cleo's feelings went, now that I had explained how she felt a lot of the pieces of the jigsaw fell into place. Lisa and I discussed what she needed to change to improve their relationship. Lisa had relaxed already and could see that a journey was about to be taken not only for Cleo but also for herself.

A month later I went out to see Cleo again and was so pleased to see the change in both the horse and Lisa. Cleo's coat now shone, she was so relaxed, feeling secure and safe, a feeling that she had not felt for a long time. As a result I could almost say the same about Lisa her complexion was glowing and the smile huge as she led me down to the field. Both Lisa and Cleo have found a way to move forward in their relationship, it hasn't all been plain sailing there have been 3 steps forward and 2 back.

But they are getting there and along the way both have changed, Lisa now listens to her inner voice and trusts her own instincts and has started to train as a healer with me. The other day Lisa said that it wouldn't matter if she never rode Cleo again the relationship and learning journey that they are both on is worth so much more.

TAMARA

Another weaning that I was called out to was not brutal but very sad; I received a phone call from a lady called Jane who was very upset. Her beloved mare Ash had had colic in the night, she had been rushed to the Equine Hospital leaving her 4 month old foal behind. But unfortunately the vets had been unable to save her and Ash had died on the operating table. Jane was obviously very upset about her mare, also very worried about the foal and she asked me to come and see the foal to see if I could help her in anyway.

Jane is a very experienced horse lady and has a beautiful yard with ten of her own horses living on her doorstep. Although upset beyond words she had managed to pull herself together and had taken the advice of her vet, the foal was being fed and cared for and when I arrived was out in the field grazing with Jane's old mare. I stood by the gate and watched as Jane went to the foal that she told me was called Tamara. When Jane had reassured the foal and put on the head collar I slowly walked towards the foal, she was very nervous. So I stopped and knelt on the ground reducing my energy and holding my hands out to her. I stayed like this for quite a while telling Tamara that I was not going to hurt her. After a while Tamara had settled and I slowly moved towards her until she was happy for me to be closer. I gently placed my hands on her shoulder and directed the healing energy into her, the wave of confusion, sadness and a feeling of being lost was immense, I let the tears of her emotion wash down my face. Tam lowered her head and relaxed and took a big breath, she started to lick and chew and we stayed like this for a while with her accepting the healing and relaxing.

Then I heard a voice in my head "over there" I looked down to the end of the field and could see nothing. Then it came again "over there" I turned and asked Jane what was over there at the end of the field she replied "nothing" suddenly the breeze got up and the other nine horses in the surrounding paddocks screamed and galloped in the opposite direction. "No it's over there" I said," what is over there?" I asked pointing in the direction the horses had bolted. "That is where Ash is buried it's the grave". I looked at the mound of earth where Ash was buried and could feel her energy; her spirit had not yet passed. She needed to make sure her foal was alright, I explained this to Jane who I could see could not quite believe what she was witnessing and hearing. I gave her a moment to get her thoughts together and told her that she had to let the foal and the other horses visit the grave. The mare needed to say goodbye. When Jane brought the foal in that night they walked to the grave the foal pawed the ground and breathed heavily over the grave, she reared and whinnied licked and chewed and was then ready to go in.

All the other horses were allowed to visit the grave some pawing the ground some breathing very heavily over the grave, they all had different reactions. The herd had been very close and they were all grieving and by letting them do this they were accepting that Ash had gone.

Tamara went to the grave two nights running and on the third came straight in, Ash had crossed over.

Because of the understanding way that the death of Tamara's mother was handled, letting her visit the grave and giving her time, Tamara has grown up with no ill effects of this sad weaning, for others they would not have been so lucky. Tamara was adopted by another mare in the herd and has grown up secure and emotionally balanced.

FEN

I received a call from a lady called Marion who had heard about my work and phoned and asked if I would treat her horse Fen. I arrived on a very happy yard the sun was shining and the place was full of energy. I introduced myself to Marion and we decided to make the most of the weather and to do the healing in the field. Marion put the head collar on Fen and I watched the two of them together, I could see that Fen had huge trust in Marion but when she saw me her eye changed. I held my hand out to Fen and told her I would not hurt her, Fen's eyes were locked on me, she backed off and was not at all happy with me being near her. I backed off and told her we had all the time in the world and started to send healing from a distance. I directed the energy from my hands so that she could become used to my energy. Which, for some horses can be very confusing!

I talked to Fen all the time very slowly moving forward and placed my hand near her shoulder; Fen immediately became aggressive and tried to bite me. Marion was shocked, but I reassured her it was fine, Fen had aggression locked in her body and I would try and heal through the block. I told Fen it was ok and that I was not going to hurt her, I lowered my energy and slowed my breathing, she let out a sigh and I slowly felt down her left side. As I moved towards her hind quarters she kicked out, so I returned to where she was happy by her shoulder. The emotion that I felt from Fen was anxiety in the pit of my stomach verging on panic.

I stayed up by her shoulder and took it very slowly, you can only offer healing in a way that it will be accepted, with Fen it was very slowly. I continued healing her and the feelings intensified until she showed me the pictures of being weaned from her mum. There was no gentle weaning, when she was taken from her Mum they had been in a stable together, when the door opened Fen went forward to have a look and they grabbed her. The stable door was banged behind her, her Mum was screaming and crashing against the door. She showed me a picture of the stable with both doors shut, Fen was calling and calling but all the time being pulled away until she showed me a picture of her inside a trailer. At the end of her journey Fen too was put into a stable with top and bottom door shut. It was dark and the whole process had been much too brutal for Fen to cope with. Fen felt very afraid and anxious and incredibly bewildered, leading to intense sadness. She hated being shut in and in my body I felt the sensation it was panic and claustrophobic. She tried to get back to her mum and escape but she was kicked in the side of her belly to make her go back, she showed me this by asking for healing in the area, as I placed my hand on the area I saw the boot making contact with her side.

During the healing, Fen tried to bite me many times, we had to work through her layers of anxiety and anger to get to the cause, which was the brutal weaning, once we got to the root she calmed and accepted the healing. Her eyes became heavy and she relaxed. Her owner cried the mare's tears a release for both of them.
I moved to her hindquarters where she again showed her anxiety by trying to kick me! I could feel huge amounts of energy and asked whether she had reared I felt that something again had panicked her and I feel that she would have reared up trying to get away. Fen was not showing me anything else about the situation but her reaction was panic and fear. I discussed this with Marion and there had been an incident when Fen was left in the care of someone else and was micro-chipped. When Marion returned Fen was very distressed, Fen relies on Marion for security and something happening without her around is too much for her to cope with. After talking about this Fen started to relax again and I finished off healing her head and she then let all the anxiety go with some of the biggest yawns ever!!

The way in which Fen was weaned has affected her greatly, she has little confidence in life and becomes stressed about a lot of things. If anxiety is present then the world is seen as a terrifying place even if it is something she has seen before, if she is feeling anxious then everything looks different and she becomes scared. Panic and flight mode kick in and she is then difficult to reach and all sense of calmness is forgotten.

If a horse has had a traumatic experience in their lives it can be shown as anger, bad behavior, stable vices i.e. cribbing, all of which people have ways of dealing with. But very few will find out why these started in the first place. You need to go back to the beginning for them to voice how they feel and let the emotion out. Then and only then can you hope to recapture the horse they would have been had man not interfered.

LILLY

I was booked to go and see a mare on the edge of the New Forest, when I arrived I found a beautiful yard with mares and foals grazing by a lake. I was going to treat a horse which was kept on livery there, her name was Lilly, her owner Sue had called me because she had a need to understand Lilly and to build a better relationship with her. Sue had not owned Lilly for long, she is 18 years old, an Irish Draft and has a tendency to be a little withdrawn and could be very strong in hand.

The yard was quite busy so we decided to take Lilly into the school where it was quiet and less distracting. I explained to Sue what I was going to do, I scanned Lilly over with my hand. When I do this I feel energy, heat, tension etc all along the body and these are all areas that I need to work on. As I was feeling Lilly over she opened a conversation with me "I have had a foal" there was a lot of anger in her voice and I asked her if she would like to talk about it. She then showed me a picture of a dead foal on the ground, it didn't look like it had gone full term. Lilly was very angry they had not let her touch the foal, it had just been taken away and she had been left as if nothing had happened. Ladies, imagine you gave birth to a still born baby, you are not allowed to touch it, to feel the soft skin and smell its own special smell, it was just taken, you were given your clothes and told to get on with your life. How would you feel? Not only then but in months and years to come, the feelings, emotions would be the same to a horse. They carry their foals for 11 months they feel them grow, the first kick they feel the milk in their udder ready to feed their young, but Lilly's foal had been taken, the only memory she had was of it dead on the ground. The people had not let her sniff the foal, had they have done so Lilly would have sensed the loss of energy and that there was nothing that she could have done.

While we were talking about the foal I was directing healing into her shoulder, where all the anxiety, grief and anger was being held causing pain and stiffness. For a while Lilly accepted the healing and relaxed and licked and chewed as the healing did it's work. Lilly then became alert as she communicated a scene to me by showing me pictures; it was a scene of men brutally trying to get a stallion to mount her. All the anger she was feeling was being directed at the men and the stallion, she kicked and kicked there was no way that she was going to let them put her in foal. During this time Lilly's owner Sue was crying Lilly's tears, she could not believe the emotion that had overcome her and I told her to let the tears fall. As she did this Lilly was yawning and releasing all the pent up emotions that she had been holding in her body. Lilly has a problem with people touching her back legs, this is as a result of the treatment that she had received during this time. She showed me that they had resorted to using hobbles on her so that she could not kick the stallion. To hobble a horses legs is to take away its survival mode, in the wild the horses flight ability keeps them safe, to have their legs chained together stopping their natural instinct is not only barbaric but cruel. The result being that the horse will be difficult with a farrier, and not like having their hind legs touched, in general they will always be on their guard and would have to learn to trust again. The mares need calm and kind treatment to regain their confidence, unfortunately this is not always done and people see it as a behavioral problem. The result of which is more brutal handling and mistreatment until the horse is labeled as a "problem horse". This is what has happened with Lilly and she had ended up at a dealers, Lilly had become very dominant she had learnt to fight, sometimes this was met by anger and violence or by being thrown out in a field and left alone until sold on again.

Lilly has spent her life being picked up and put down; nobody has understood her or helped her until now. Sue had bought Lilly from a dealer but at the time was not experienced enough to deal with Lillie's problems so had listened to other people's advice. We have all been there when someone much more experienced than us offers advice, you think they must be right when all the time there is your little inner voice trying to come out and say "WAIT". As a result of this they were both going round in circles. Lilly with mistrust, panic and hate, Sue not knowing who to listen to, she was feeling huge guilt and also a failure, she felt that she had failed Lilly. Unfortunately, too many people think that horses problems can be beaten out of them when in fact they need the opposite. They need kindness and reassurance time after time until they realise they can trust.

Now that Sue understands why Lilly behaves in the way that she does they are working together to form a better relationship. Starting with a change of home, the sight of all the foals is too much for Lilly, so a new yard has been found and their relationship is becoming stronger. When mares have been abused both mentally and physically they will remember and it goes on to play a huge part of their lives. Leading to being misunderstood, which can as a result scare people, a dominant angry mare can be very vicious and if you come back at them with strong tactics they will come back with even stronger ones. Never underestimate the anger of an abused mare, years of patience love and understanding is needed, some fall into the right hands but for many others the abuse carries on until the problem becomes so big they are put to sleep.

All of these horses have been affected by the bond between mother and foal being broken. The mare and foal feel the same emotions as people; the only difference is that they do not have a voice.

People think that horses do not feel and yet as I have found horses can develop behavioral problems during their lives as a result of a cruel weaning. Their anger can come out at a later time when more is being asked of them, they remember the intense emotional pain and it comes out in their behavior. They will be seen to be a "problem horse" stronger handling and gadgets will be used when all they had to do is ask why, what has caused the horse to behave in such a way……

4

WHAT IS HEALING

History is full of stories about horses having played a key part in our civilisation. From fighting wars with us, pulling the plough to enable us to grow our crops they have been beside us helping us in our lives. We owe them a huge debt for better or worse they have helped us change the world.

A straight forward definition of healing is

"to restore health"

Dictionary definition; "the process of making or becoming sound or healthy again:*the gift of healing"*

To me it is also showing love, understanding and accepting the horse for who they are and voicing their voice, so that those close to them have a chance of understanding.

If you understand why your horses behave the way they do, it gives you a chance to work with them and accept them as they are or perhaps for you to change, so that your relationship improves. The horse is slowly being heard and every horse I see and communicate with is another horse drawing their person nearer to them to have a bond they knew was possible but thought might never happen.

The therapy of healing using hands is one of the oldest forms of medicine; ancient drawings show the laying of hands on people. It is not some new age fashionable therapy but a form of healing that goes back a long way and some say is the 'true healing'. Placing the hands on a body – human or animal is often called 'spiritual healing' there are no symbols or rituals and no one can lay claim to it. For the act of healing is within us all, I believe we are all born with the healing ability to help and love others.

Within every living being lies the spirit of the body, it is an oscillating field of energy, healing aims to direct a flow of this life force and there by release negative energy and restore balance. Where there is a problem in the body, blockages occur in the energy field and the body becomes out of rhythm. We are not just talking about physical conditions, a lot of energy blocks are caused by emotional issues which need to be released and healed. For the horse these blocks can cause aches and pains within the body, shortness of stride, lameness and also behavioral problems.

The Benefits of Healing Horses

Healing can be used for all conditions and has no adverse side effects, however healing does not take the place of a vet and your vet should always be contacted and permission asked for before a healing takes place.

Healing reaches throughout the physical body as well as the mental and emotional state.

Healing is a natural therapy and works with the individual horses body.

Healing may be able to succeed where all else has failed.

Healing can be used preventatively

Healing produces a feeling of inner calm and peacefulness.

More importantly, with healing and communication it gives the horse a chance to be heard. When their issues are discussed and the emotions released and the area healed the problems can be resolved.

I am not a horse whisperer, yes I have psychic ability and aided by my guides I act as a funnel for healing energy. With my ability to communicate with the horse I restore the balance to their body which has been distorted by humans or their life in general. I have the ability to connect directly with a horse's mind, "impossible" I hear the skeptics shout, the rest of this book will hopefully make you want to think again.

There is a lot to be learnt from 'The Horse' we could learn ways that would greatly improve our lives and yet we choose to dominate these beautiful spirited animals. Mankind thinks they know best but if I achieve nothing else with writing this book I hope it may make you think again. Through my healing sessions with the horse I have been shown horrifying pictures of cruelty, both physically and mentally. As their stories unfold I ask myself again and again, why? Does the human race think they are so clever that they have nothing to learn, that they know it all. No, mostly it is ignorance, they don't know or realise what a horse could show or teach them.

Perhaps this is why people choose not to listen because they will not like what they are told and feelings will have to be confronted. Have we become so far removed that we are beyond learning? For some yes but others the door is starting to open and people are waking up to themselves and consequently to their horses.

Many people are telling me that the horse they have in their lives is not the horse they went to look at but it is a horse that called to them. Even when they were trying the horse they went to buy they could feel the eyes of another boring into their soul. The question had to be asked, can I have a look at that one over there and sure enough the horse they bring home is the one who called them.

Once taken home the owners have gone on a roller coaster ride with the horse, usually when they think they cannot cope anymore I get a phone call. My visit is quite often the last chance the horse has, this can be a powerful healing for both horse and owner as the details come out as to why the person was chosen. It is so the horse can connect with the owner and carry out their own healing on them. When that horse called from the other side of the yard and connected with you he saw a mirror of a wounded spirit. He could relate to your energy and the emotions that are held within and need to be let out. As I voice this, the owner's tears fall and a beautiful joint healing takes place. The owners have felt the connection but chose to ignore it and stay in their safe and unfeeling world. For others they know the horse is trying to connect with them but become confused as to what the message is. Together through me the horse can communicate with their owner they can tell them exactly how they feel and how the owner's inner energy and emotions affect them.

Healings like this start off a whole new change of direction for the owners, they start to listen. They become keen to change and learn from the horse a new way of being, this will have a knock on affect throughout their lives. They will become more understanding of not just their horse but of everyone around them, they will find out who they really are. So the horses are bringing about their own form of healing, things are changing for them and not before time.

When I was training with Bill he used to give me readings to help me with my work, during one reading he told me I would be teaching healing to others. I can remember laughing and telling him he must be joking, but here I am years later teaching others the beauty of Equine Healing and Communication. As I teach my students and they tell their children what they are doing the children are opening themselves up to a better understanding of the horse, so a new generation is being reached.

When I eventually came "out of the closet" as I call it and stood proudly, and said I am a healer and I talk to horses I can honestly say it was the best thing I ever did. By declaring it to everyone who would listen I developed a backbone and confidence to go forward and help the horses. It is not something I did lightly but something I am so glad I did and through my work we are making people listen not only to their horses but to themselves. Through healing and communication the horses are being heard and it is amazing watching the transformation of both horse and people being healed.

5

"THE PROBLEM HORSE"

He is a "problem horse," this is a label given to many when nobody has listened, is a horse born a problem? My answer is no.

> They come into this world as beautiful free spirits with so much knowledge in the first seconds of life.

Foals are born with an ability to quickly escape predators; normally a foal will stand up and feed within the first hour of being born. They can trot and canter within hours and most can gallop by the next day, so where does the "problem horse" originate from?

I am of the belief that man causes "problem horses," we fail to listen, how many times have you ignored the kick, the buck, the rear, the bolt etc. These are the first signs of communication from your horse that something is wrong. Do we ask what? no, more often than not harder training methods are used or the horse is "taught a lesson". If you take on a horse that is trying to tell you something is wrong he will either fight back and things can become quite nasty or he will become depressed and withdraw inside himself. Same as people really, anger fuels anger and is not the answer. To me a problem arises when no one listens, when there is a communication breakdown..........

HARLEY

One of my earlier clients that I was called to was a horse called Harley, he had been brought from the auctions for a teenager to ride and since arriving home they had been unable to do anything with him. Everything was difficult, from catching him, leading, tacking up and if you managed to get on he would buck until you were off.

I arrived at the yard where he was kept and introduced myself; Pam his owner led me to his stable. As I approached the stable I could feel Harley's negative energy towards me, it was leaping off the walls'. Pam put on his head collar and I entered his stable, his reaction to me was very violent and had I stayed in his stable I would have been kicked or had his teeth in my arm! Harley could sense my energy and knew that I was different and there was no way he was going to let me near him. I explained what was happening and reassured Pam that it was ok. I scanned his body over the door, Harley's skin was tight across his skeleton and was very dull, there was no healthy shine and his eye was haunted. I felt his body was holding emotion after emotion and somewhere deep inside was a frightened Harley.

I explained to Pam that Harley had been through an awful lot in his life and it was not going to be a quick fix, it could take weeks to unravel as he was so traumatised. Pam didn't care she just wanted to understand what was making Harley behave like this.

I started of the first session healing him over the stable door at a distance because this was where he was happy for me to be. I worked on my breathing and reducing my body energy so that he didn't think I was there to challenge him. During the session he started to relax and accept healing, the first few sessions were carried out in this way until Harley was happy for me to enter his stable. I carried on healing from a distance slowly moving forward, as I was getting closer I could see the healing was being accepted and he was becoming more relaxed.

On the fourth visit Harley let me place my hand on his shoulder he remained relaxed and I carried on sending the healing energy from my hand into his body. The longer Harley stayed with me the more relaxed he became. I slowly started moving my hand over his body, he would soon let me know if I went too far and I would move my hand back. The healing and energy release was done at a speed that Harley could cope with. I was allowed to touch his shoulders and the front of his body but not his face. I worked on these areas over the next couple of sessions but at no time was I allowed near his head or hind quarters, this was fine, Harley was becoming more and more relaxed in my company and was now looking to greet me over the door when I arrived!

On my 6th visit I asked Pam if we could take him out of the stable for his healing and she led him into the sunshine. When I saw Harley that day I knew that he was going to open up and release and I wanted him to be in a bigger area to be able to do this. I started healing on his shoulder as normal and then worked my way down his back, he became quite agitated and we moved around the yard, I asked him if he wanted to continue and he said "yes". I was on his left-side now with my hand on his ribs when he showed me in pictures his story; I saw a horse in very poor condition, he was skin and bone. Harley was feeling very weak and he had no energy to move, my mouth became dry as I felt his thirst he had not had a good drink in a long while. There were a lot of horses around him all on high alert and panicking and there were men shouting. Harley was being loaded onto a lorry, the men were shouting at him and the air was filled with an energy which scared Harley. There were lots of horses being loaded and the atmosphere was filled with anger and very intense. Harley was with a group of horses and as he got on the ramp he stumbled and fell onto his side, he tried to get up but he was so weak his energy had gone. The men were shouting and kicking him, the boots hit every part of his body then one of the men started using a whip on him to make him move. Whilst Harley was communicating with me we were walking around the yard, Pam suddenly gasped and said "look," down the side of Harley the whip marks were raised on his coat and we could see where the stinging whip had connected with his skin. He eventually found the energy to stand and he was forced into the lorry.

 As he was telling his story his eyes became heavy and then he started to lick and chew as the energy held in his body was released, followed by the biggest yawns. I carried on healing Harley, the stress and trauma that had been held in his body needed healing through. Harley became very sleepy and when I finished he let me stroke his head for the first time. This was beautiful he was so relaxed probably more relaxed than he had been in years.

 For a horse to release a deep rooted memory when it is as bad as this is a huge thing and Harley now needed time to absorb the healing energy and to heal the wounds inside. Harley had been the victim of a very brutal and cruel life; he was in pain throughout his body from the deep stress and tension held from his life. He could not cope with people riding him because his back hurt, he was not playing up, testing them or being naughty but in pain.

After this healing Harley was a lot brighter and much happier to see people. He still had problems in his body due to the way that he was treated and starved, his back had been checked and found to be very weak and his owners decided to keep him as a companion for their other horse rather than try and ride him, a decision I was very happy with.

By telling his story Harley was able to be understood and also to release the emotions held in his body, from this experience his back became softer. Locked in emotion leads to tension in the body muscle causing spasm and lameness, to try and help the horse you need to firstly acknowledge the experience and release the tension held.

FROSTY

I received a call from Dawn who owns a local horse rehabilitation yard near where I live in Dorset. One of her clients had recently brought an x-race horse from the auction and taken it to Dawns as a livery, Dawn and her staff were having dreadful trouble with the horse as it was very angry and was dangerous to handle.

I arrived on the yard to be introduced to Frosty who was a beautiful grey with a black mane and tail. Dawn went into the stable and put on his head collar and went to tie him up, I asked her why she was doing this as I have treated a lot of horses for Dawn and never once have we tied them up. I knew how bad things had got when she said "it would be safer". I do not like horses to be tied up when I treat them I like them to be able to move and to also be able to point out areas on their body where they wanted me to work.

I told Dawn that I would take my chances and took hold of the rope; I spoke to Frosty who was very agitated. He was so wound up and tense he couldn't stand still, his mind was all over the place, fear, flight, stay, thinking, everything. His first reaction to me was to try and bite me, barge me, kick me anything but let me near him. I decided that I needed to break down his barrier and placed my hand on his shoulder he straight away swung his head round to bite me and I blocked him with my arm.

I knew that I had to get Frosty thinking, to use his brain so I focused my energy on his hind quarters so that he kept them away from me. We carried on moving around the box with me in control using my body energy but in a way another horse would. Slowly, slowly, his energy came down and I reduced mine until he became calm and licked and chewed and let me stroke him. I passed his rope to Dawn and stroked down his body with my hands, he had dreadful heat in his shoulder, wither and spine and for today I was not going near the hind legs. I passed all this information onto Dawn and said that he had had enough for today, he would now be easier for them to handle and that I would be back in a week to carry out a healing session on his body.

The following week I returned to see Frosty again he was much more relaxed and pleased to see me. Dawn said that he had been a good boy and they had managed to lead him in and out to the field safely. His owner had done some digging and found out that he had been in quite a few racing yards but never been raced.

Frosty was indeed a different horse, I stroked his neck and shoulder and told him that we would work at his pace. He straight away relaxed and started licking and chewing and I slowly moved my hand towards his wither. Under my hand the heat was radiating out of his body, it was like a heater. I left my hand there and Frosty turned his head and looked at me, I asked him if he was alright and he replied "yes" and told me that he wanted to carry on.

Frosty then showed me pictures, there was an angry man riding him and Frosty was bucking and bucking there was pain and he couldn't stand the man on top of him. The man was shouting at him and whipping him until Frosty reared up and went over backwards the man fell clear but Frosty went over backwards smashing his wither on the ground. There was no rest and treatment for Frosty the torture continued they kept trying to work him and Frosty did all that he could to communicate with them that he was in pain.

Nobody would listen, man was fueling their ego and they were determined to control Frosty, and as a result of this he received lots of severe beatings from angry men. Then I could see a rope fastened to his bridle. One part went round his body behind his shoulders and some how this was attached to his bridle, but I could not see what he was showing me so I asked him again. He grabbed hold of the sleeve of my coat and pulled my arm between his front legs, to show me where the rope went, they then pulled and pulled on the rope until he crashed to the floor onto his right shoulder. He kept showing me the picture and his fear which turned into anger over what they were doing to him. I carried on healing Frosty and cried his tears, he could not understand why they would not listen. He was in intense pain every time they got into the saddle the pain was too much. When Frosty had relaxed he became very sleepy he yawned as the energy shifted in his body and I knew he had had enough for today.

I then turned to Dawn who had been watching the anger, stress and tears and I translated to her what they all meant. I told Dawn what I had been shown and she said that she had heard of it before it is a method used to break the horses spirit, with the rope connected like that if he keeps on fighting there is no where for him to go except to fall.

I said to Dawn that I was very worried about his back and wither and that she should get Anita the physio to take a look. Anita was booked the following week and I met her at the yard as Frosty was still nervous around people he didn't know. I managed to keep him quiet so that she could examine him, she gave him a treatment and then came back a week later. She was not happy as there had been no change and it was decided to have his back x-rayed. The results of the x-ray showed that Frosties spine was damaged and had fused together creating pain when ridden. This is why Frosty behaved as he did he wasn't naughty or disobedient or needed to be taught a lesson but in agonising pain.

The decision was made to put Frostie to sleep so that nobody else would try and ride him. Frosty was 5 years old he had been through so much in his short life and none of it was good. People have to change their way of thinking, drop the ego and ask "why", because until we do more and more horses will end up the same way as Frosty.

Rest in Peace Frosty you are safe from mankind now……………x

The story you have just read is true and factual, it is the horses own story of his short life. A life full of ill treatment that he had received due to him being labeled a "problem horse" Frosties problem was that he was in intense pain but nobody listened.

Communication between humans and animals is not a fantasy or wistful dream it really happens in varying degrees and levels; it is achievable by every one of us. My approach is different from the work of many people referred to as "horse whisperers". My work is not about dominating horses, but understanding them, to work together. To bring about an end to some of the horrific training methods used to break the horses spirit and do as man instructs.

I work at another level where I communicate directly with the horses mind, work with the energy within and surrounding all living things. Some people are able to make this connection more easily than others and I am lucky to be one of them. I say to everyone I meet that we all have this ability when we are born, but as life goes on it is a sense within us that is not nurtured but closed and forgotten.

How do animals communicate with me? in many different ways. With some horses I have wonderful conversations just like I would with a friend, some find it easier to express their communication in pictures, with the communication comes sensations and feelings in my body. I then translate as accurately as I can the message I receive.

Sometimes there is no inner voice or pictures, just the feeling in my body and the horses emotions. If they are sad my tears fall, if it's anger, I voice the anger, by using my hands I feel where the horse is holding the experience or anxiety within their body and I work on this area to release it. The only way I can describe it is the way people hold tension in their bodies, often the shoulders which in turn affects the neck and back if not released. The same is true for horses you can have a physio or back person out but if the experience and emotion is not released the tension will return.

There are many people who remain skeptical about the validity of my work. Showing as it does that horses feel love, pain, fear, anger, joy, jealousy, guilt, grief, and all the other emotions that make up our human repertoire, and with many, also a fantastic sense of humor. For some people crediting a horse with human emotions poses no particular problem, but for many it makes them feel uncomfortable to think about how they would feel if they had the same treatment as their horse…….

TJ

I was phoned by my friend Sarah who is a dressage rider, she had brought a horse from Germany and was having problems with him and booked me to go and see him.

TJ is a big 18hh Warmblood, Sarah was having problems riding TJ his concentration was zero and as she was getting firmer with him the more dangerous he was becoming. He could not concentrate his mind for long enough to do a dressage test and she did not know what to do with him.

As I entered the yard a voice called out to me "Good morning to you" in a beautiful Irish accent. "To be sure to be sure" I looked around the yard and saw this big beautiful grey gazing at me over the stable door. I said "hello" to him and went to find Sarah so that she could introduce me to her German horse.

I was very surprised when Sarah led me to my Irish friend, he had the cheekiest eye and that gorgeous Irish Accent. I was lost for words - not like me at all! I double checked with Sarah that he was German and she confirmed that he had been bred in Germany so I turned my attentions to TJ. I asked him if I could treat him and he was quite happy to have the attention, he was very chatty and continued to speak to me with his Irish accent, not a hint of German anywhere. I felt over his body and as I scanned him and chatted to him I asked why the Irish, he said it was all he knew, it was how his groom had spoken to him. Just goes to show never judge the book by the cover! Just because he came from Germany don't necessarily expect a German.

I felt a lot of heat in TJ's shoulder which I started working on and he relaxed and absorbed the healing energy. I carried on down through his back and found it all to be tender and uncomfortable, I could feel heat down his front legs then my eyes were drawn to his hind legs. I ran my hands down them and Sarah warned "careful he may kick" which he did quite violently. I healed his legs from a distance and could see marks coming up in his hair around the fetlock area. He showed me pictures of his legs being hobbled – tied together - I asked him why they had done this and he showed me a picture of him bucking and rearing. Whilst I was healing and communicating with him whip marks also showed on his body as in TJ's words "he was taught a lesson". "Did it work?" I asked him "no" he replied "had no respect for them I gave back as good as they gave me." I healed him through this event in his life and he licked and chewed and yawned, I told him that I wanted to help him and I would return next week to give him another healing session.

Because of the treatment that TJ had had in Germany and

because of his strong personality he became hard and unwilling to learn, anger was mirrored with anger a very vicious and dangerous circle. Sarah persevered with him and I continued to provide healing, it was during one of our healing sessions that I was drawn to his front legs, as I ran my hand down his legs I felt a dull ache in mine. I placed my hands on the area and asked him what the problem was? "It's the ground it is hard and hurts my legs." Sarah confirmed that to try and get TJ's interest they had been jumping him out in the field. I told her there was a problem with the leg and I got the impression it was something to do with the bone. The vet was called and x-rays carried out which showed that he did have a bony growth in his leg, it could not be operated on and hard work and hard ground would affect it.

Sarah is a dressage rider and TJ had been her dream horse, he had the breeding to go far and this had been her intention to compete him in dressage. Unfortunately due to the hard handling that he had received at such a young age, his strong character and his injuries this was not going to happen. There is a lesson here for everyone; time and time again I come across horses that are bred to race or do dressage etc. I point out to people that my father may have been a brain surgeon this does not mean that I would be one to. Horses are the same, so much pressure is put on them to perform when in fact the horse that they are can not cope with the discipline.   This now put Sarah in a difficult position, she thought long and hard about what to do with TJ it was obvious that he was not going to be a dressage horse due to his mentality and also the problem with his legs. It was then that she had a phone call from a friend asking her if she knew of a horse that would make a good hack for an experienced rider. Sarah mentioned TJ and the lady came out and tried him, she laughed at his behavior in the school and said that she had no intention of schooling him. She lived near the beach and he would be hacked down onto the beach for long canters. The going would be perfect for his legs, Sarah was very pleased and TJ was taken to his new home where he still is now. He still comes to me in meditations every so often and tells me how he is doing in that lovely Irish accent.

BOW

Another horse of Sarah's called Bow was given to Sarah to compete, he was an advance dressage horse and Sarah was very excited to have the opportunity of riding him. Bow's owner had had him since he was a foal but her work was taking her abroad and she wanted him to go to a loving home where he could carry on with his dressage career.

Bow arrived at Sarah's and It wasn't long before I had a call to go out and see him, Bow was not happy, Sarah was finding it difficult to build a relationship with him and this was showing in his work. I went out and met Bow who was indeed not very happy, during our healing session he showed me his old life and his wonderful owner, he blamed Sarah for taking him away from everything that he knew. I told him that his owner could no longer keep him and he had been given to Sarah because she could provide a lovely home for him.

Bow was a very sad and confused horse, he had been with his owner since he was a foal and they had a wonderful relationship and then suddenly that all changed and he was not coping. He was going through the same trauma as a ten year old child who is suddenly adopted, confused, angry, lashing out, throwing blame anywhere and every where. Sarah phoned me a few days later and said she could not reach him and was thinking of phoning Bow's owner about the problem as she would hate for him to be unhappy. I said to wait and I would call in, by the time I arrived it was dark and very stormy.

I asked Sarah to come into the stable with me, I said hello to Bow and asked him if I could open a connection between him and Sarah and would he listen. He agreed so I explained to Sarah that I would place my hand on Bow's shoulder and my other hand on her shoulder and I needed her to place her hand on his neck. I guided Sarah through the opening of the communication channel and asked them, through me, to talk. Sarah felt a bit silly at first until she heard it, Bow's voice, he told her how he felt, that she had taken him away from his owner. She explained to him that his owner had to go away and how she wanted to give him a loving home and that his owner would call in from time to time. Sarah told him how she had a lot to learn from him and asked to be given a chance. Bow thought about this for a moment and agreed to try, they then remained connected and exchanged energy to bond the relationship.

Sarah was amazed and could not believe what had happened; I explained that if she did what we had just done Bow would communicate with her so there should be no further misunderstandings.

Bow and Sarah went onto have a wonderful dressage life together and Sarah did learn from him, at 21 he was about to retire when he was hit by colic and had to be put to sleep. He was a beautiful horse who opened Sarah's eyes not only to top level dressage but also to how changes can affect horses and how by listening and communicating problems can be overcome.

LEO

I was booked to treat a horse called Leo in Wimborne, it was a beautiful summer's day and we decided to treat him out in the field. I introduced myself to Leo and he was very laid back and relaxed and started licking and chewing before I had even started. He was happy in my energy but would not let me use the pendulum near him, he didn't need it. I must tell you about Leo he is the most amazing colour, black with silver which in the sun gave of a beautiful aqua green aura it is amazing. He is a Uruguayan Criollo, a breed that I had never heard of before.

I felt Leo over and was pleased with how relaxed he was, He then started talking to me and showing me some of his life. I saw him in a big herd with his mum, he was happy, then the feeling changed to fear. I could see him being rounded up and the youngsters secured in a coral it looked like something out of a Western movie. The horses were left frightened and scared it was a hot day there was no food or water and I was hit with an intense thirst. He then showed me how the men appeared at the coral with ropes and one by one they were lassoed and pulled to the ground. My attention was taken to his sheath and he showed me the horses being pulled to the ground and gelded, no sedation just manhandled and job done it was a horrible sight. I gave his sheath area healing and be licked and chewed and yawned as he released the blocked energy held in his body.

The horses then appeared to be in a barn, Leo stood quietly at the back watching what was happening, a lot of the horses were scared and fighting with their handlers. Resulting in the horses being beaten, Leo took all of this in and realised if he did as he was told his life would be easier and he would stand more of a chance of surviving. The backing process was brutal nothing gradual, bridle, blanket, and saddle and expected to work straight away, again he did as he was told. He found the work too fast and furious and as he was telling me this his breathing became more rapid as he was releasing the memory. I let him have a rest and asked him if he wanted to continue, he did. He then showed me horses being loaded onto what I thought must be a lorry, some of them were very poor and you could see their bones, if they hesitated they were whipped and then the door was closed. I then felt they were left for a long time and again I had a dreadful thirst there was no water. Leo's owner explained that it was not a lorry but a ship they were transported to Holland a journey lasting weeks and only the strongest survived. Those that could walk off the boat did and the rest were thrown overboard. He continued licking and chewing, his eyes were heavy and he was releasing the emotions of the event by yawning.

My attention was then drawn to his right knee as I placed my hand on the knee I could feel heat from an old injury. As I sent healing to the area I asked Leo what had caused the injury, he showed me the first part of the backing process was to tie the front leg up and leave them struggling to move around on three legs. As they became more and more tired the men would watch them and when exhaustion was taking over their bodies they would untie the leg throw on the saddle and ride them. It is a very old method used in other countries which is very cruel. I told his owner about the injury and how it had happened. She confirmed that the leg had been treated by the vet and that there was damage to the leg and now arthritis was setting in.

Leo is the most amazing horse, he has been through so much and yet he is a survivor and gives so much to his owner they have a beautiful partnership and it is wonderful to see.

VICTOR

I received an email from a lady called Amie requesting a visit to her horse called Victor who she had owned for a few months but could not make out why he seemed so unhappy and miserable all the time.

I travelled down to Devon and went to visit Amie and Victor, when I arrived Victor was tied up outside his shelter and as Amie and I talked he completely ignored us. I asked Amie to hold Victor's rope as I introduced myself and scanned his body. By asking the owner to hold their horse I learn an awful lot about their relationship. I spoke to Victor and placed my hand on his shoulder he started walking around and then barged into Amie. I decided it would be better to go into Victor's stable as we had some anger issues to go through and I felt he needed to be in a safer environment.

Victor had been brought at the auction by his previous owner and none of his history was known. I started scanning his body and found huge amounts of energy locked in on his left side so I started healing on the right. To start with he was not very happy in my company, he had a lot of anger in his energy and had survived like this for a long time, it had become his barrier I needed to find a hole in it if I was going to help him.

When he eventually became quiet and I started healing him he showed me the time when he was with his mum, he had a wonderful relationship with her and the herd. He showed me the herd running free in a huge area. There was no dreadful weaning it was done naturally as nature intended, then it all changed, it seemed that as soon as humans got involved his anger started. He had been totally misunderstood, he could not cope with all that was being asked of him and the pressure had been immense and made him angry. Because of his anger and the way it caused him to behave people in the past had given up on him, he has been picked up and put down so many times over his 6 years of life that he has almost given up trying.

Whilst he was telling me this he was getting more and more agitated and pulling his owner round the stable. I took hold of the rope and carried on healing him, some of the time walking in circles as I worked until he calmed down and relaxed. I felt that he lacked confidence and I could see a picture of someone riding him and he wanted them to relax. When I mentioned this to his owner she said that it was possibly her as she lacked confidence after a fall, so I explained that he wanted her to relax and he would look after her. He told me he hated being lunged and with his stiffness he found it difficult, which is why he then became naughty. Amie confirmed that she had given up lunging him because he would buck and try and change direction all the time. I explained to her that this was due to pain in his body caused by the tension running through his left side. This would make it very difficult for him to work on the right rein.

Victor then became very quiet and accepted the healing, his energy reduced and his body relaxed he then did the biggest stretch I have ever seen. He arched his neck and back and released all the pent up emotion held in his body, he then laid down and I carried on healing him as he snored. Being angry and miserable all the time can make the body very tired and releasing it left the body needing to rest.

The healing has enabled Amie to understand him and they are working together to make Victor a happy boy and to stop him holding onto stress in his body. They have built on their relationship, both now enjoying each other's company and Amie has been hunting on him this season.

I then received a phone call from Amie asking if I could visit again but this time he was at a livery yard. Amie met me in the car park and took me to Victor. As I arrived at his stable he couldn't wait for me to get started. "You're here Lainey" he said, Amie had told me that since moving to the yard his behavior had deteriorated, he had also become lame and she had stopped riding him.

I put my hands on Victor and he straight away accepted the healing, he turned round and round in his stable and then laid down and waited for me to carry on. As I healed him I could feel his anxiety, there was a lot of heat radiating from his pelvis. He was drifting off to sleep and then quickly got back onto his feet. "It's the noise, always disturbed, people coming and going" with that a piece of roofing banged in the wind. "You see" I turned to Amie and told her that Victor is finding the yard to noisy and I felt that his hearing was very sensitive. The comings and goings of all the people disturbed him and he really wasn't settled. Victor then heard the horse in the next stable and put his ears back to show his disapproval. Amie laughed and said he doesn't like the horse next door! Victor then went down again and this time it stayed quiet enough for him to sleep. I felt intense tiredness and told Amie that he is not relaxing enough to rest and is very tired. As I healed his pelvis I felt huge sadness come over me and I could see his field where he used to be kept. I looked at Amie and told her that he was homesick for his field. Although there he was kept on his own he had settled and it had been the first place in his life that he had felt safe and secure. Amie confirmed that she had not given up the field and I suggested he go back there and then Victor would be fine.

Eventually Victor woke up and stood to his feet and I told him he would be going home! He licked and chewed and yawned as he took the information in. Two weeks later Victor returned to his field and Amie told me she had never seen a horse so happy. He galloped round and round bucking and then grazed for a while before he laid down and had a wonderful peaceful sleep.

Although a lot of horses hate being on their own for Victor it was perfect, he felt secure with just Amie around. Now that he is relaxed his back is better and they are again hacking out on the Moors.

GINGER

I was booked to see a mare in Devon, I didn't know too much about her and when I arrived I was met by a beautiful Thoroughbred. Ginger was stunning but her eye was anxious and her nerves were on red alert. As I walked towards her stable I could feel her anxiety and fear, I turned to her owner and told her that Ginger thought I had come to look at her to buy, she thought she was for sale. Laura confirmed for me that Ginger was not for sale and would never be and I told Ginger this.

When I entered the stable I stood back so that Ginger could get used to my energy and slowly started to introduce myself. When I touched her I could feel her anxiety she was like a coiled spring, grabbing pieces of hay and then crib biting on the side of the stable. I stood back and healed from a distance for a while and then placed my hand on her shoulder. When she became a little happier I was able to communicate properly and she started to accept the healing. Straight away Ginger started to communicate, she needed to off load and she showed me pictures of a very professional yard, there was a school and a walker. Ginger told me she was worked hard, she struggled with the work and mentally it was total overload. The routine was too intense and the pressure of the work was all too much too soon, she couldn't cope with the environment and people there. I told Laura what I was being shown and she confirmed that the yard where Ginger had been before she bought her was a very big college. Ginger had been very depressed and switched off, Laura had been at the college and felt that Ginger needed her and so had arranged to buy her.

Ginger continued to tell me about a fall which looked to be a cross country jump, she didn't mean to stop and for Laura to crash to the ground but she had felt a break in their connection and wasn't happy to jump. I asked Ginger what she meant by a "break in their connection". She explained that she had felt Laura doubt that they could do it so she had stopped, resulting in the fall. I told Laura about this and she confirmed that it had been their first time out and she had been nervous. I explained to her that if Ginger feels any question or lack of confidence from her she will not compete, the rider has to be 100% confident about what they are doing and then as a team they will fly.

The healing continued and Ginger's energy continued to come down she stopped walking around the stable and relaxed becoming quite sleepy and licking and chewing. Relaxing is not something that comes easy to Ginger, ever since her working life had begun she had been put under too much pressure. As a result she had switched off and become withdrawn which is why she had looked depressed when Laura had met her. Although Ginger looks like an athlete capable of big jumps, inside she is very vulnerable, thankfully her lovely owner realised this and has now provided her with a relaxed home and secure partnership. Because of the stress she holds anxiety down through her back which causes her to be stiff and if not treated, lame, her owner is aware of this and Ginger has the back lady to see her.

At the end of the healing Ginger was able to release the stress with huge yawns and was very relaxed. Later her owner told me that she had never seen her horse react to anyone in the way that Ginger had to me, I explained that she could feel my energy and it isn't everyday that someone communicates with them in the way that I do. For the very sensitive it can take a little time to get used to it.

TELA

I had been booked to visit a horse called Tela, Tela had only been with her owner Kate for 3 weeks and she was worried about the anxiety and stress that Tela was showing. As I walked into the stable Tela started grinding her teeth stretching her jaw and pawing the ground.

Once I introduced myself to Tela she relaxed a little and I placed my hand on her shoulder. I scanned her over and could feel tension within her body. The first thing Tela showed me was of her being shown in hand, she loved it, although not Arab that is what she looked like, the picture she gave to me showed her with her tail up and prancing around looking beautiful. I told Kate what I was seeing and she confirmed that the mare had had a successful showing record during the first few years of her life.

I was then very drawn to Tela's mouth, as I moved my hands near her jaw I could feel the tension and that any restriction will cause her to panic. She needs to be able to come forward into the bridle, Tela can't cope with heavy hands or being pulled into the contact. Her mouth has had a lot of firm handling which has caused huge tension in her, if the mouth is restricted with flash or firm hands her anxiety will come out in another way. Her owner confirmed that this had already started to happen if Tela is restricted with a tight rein she starts pacing on the spot and then starts too rear. I explained to Kate and her daughter that they need to ride Tela as one. Let Tela show you, ride together in harmony and not the rider as the dominant one, Tela can teach them an awful lot. If ridden forward and light she will come round and connect but you cannot force this.

Tela was also having trouble coping with the young teenagers around her and I explained that as she is so sensitive arguing near her cannot happen because she will pick up on the anger and it will cause her to become distressed. Tela needs to be in a calm and understanding environment she has been through a lot of pressure at her previous home and it will take time and reassurance to enable her to relax.

I carried on with the healing and worked down through the tension in Tela's neck and shoulders caused by her anxiety. If you clench your jaw shut feel the tension in your face and head and down through your neck and eventually into your shoulders. This is what has happened to Tela, a tight flash nose band makes the tension go all down her body. If she can move her jaw and lick and chew she will stay calmer and her body relaxed. As I worked she relaxed and licked and chewed and then yawned as the tension left her body.

As I was treating Tela I felt my breathing was becoming short and I needed to cough I felt like I had dust in my mouth which was coming from the bedding. I mentioned this to Kate who said that she had noticed Tela coughing and was going to change her bedding.

If Kate and her daughter work together slowly they will form a wonderful relationship with Tela but it will have to be slowly and quietly done, if you put Tela under pressure she will become stressed and this will show in her behaviour.

I left Kate and her daughter with a lot to think about, it can be quite a shock when you realise how much your behavior around the horses can affect them.

Flo

I received a phone call from Joy asking me to visit her rescued horse; Flo had been brought as a brood mare as her owners said she was too dangerous to ride. Joy went to see Flo and recognised a horse in need she brought her home and has spent time gaining Flo's confidence.

I arrived to meet Joy who is a tiny lady barely five feet tall and Flo an 18hh Warmblood! Joy told me that she did not know much about Flo's past and was interested in anything that Flo had to say. I explained how I worked and that I would share with her anything that Flo passed to me.

As we approached the stable Flo was looking at me and I was stunned by the depth of her eye you could see straight into her soul. Joy put Flo's head collar on and I entered the stable, Flo was not happy in my presence and became very agitated. I backed off and stood with my hands facing her with a distance of about eight feet between us. I could feel a huge barrier from Flo my hands were pinging off of her like she was surrounded with an electric current.

I spoke to Flo and told her that I was not there to hurt her and carried on healing from a distance for a while. Flo was still not happy so I put my hands in cold water to cool them down and had a word with my guides to lower my rate of healing energy it was too strong for Flo. Flo looked at me and pawed the ground, I slowly moved forward and placed my hand on her leg, she accepted the contact her skin was tight and her nerves were on edge, I kept my energy low. I slowly moved my hand to her shoulder and asked Flo if I could help her to relax. I told her we did not need to talk about anything that disturbed her I would leave it up to her but asked her to accept the healing.

I didn't move my hand anywhere else on her body as letting me touch her shoulder was a huge thing for Flo. I knew from her behavior that Flo had been through some dreadful treatment and I desperately wanted to help her. Flo relaxed enough for the healing from my hand to enter her body, there was no talking from Flo but she did start to show me pictures.

The pictures showed Flo's hind legs tied together so that she could not move and she was in the company off rough men. The men were holding her as they were trying to get a stallion to mount her. The feeling of being violated, raped, was huge, Flo hated everything that was happening to her she was being attacked and she fought with all her energy to get away and to stop it happening. The fear and anger I felt from Flo was immense and through the whole event she was more frightened than words can describe, my mouth became dry as I felt her fear, anger and panic. Exactly what a woman would feel in the same situation. My hand was shaking with the intenseness of the healing and my eyes filled with tears.

I stayed with Flo as she started to relax then she began licking and chewing as the stress left her body. When she was ready she carried on sharing her story, it seems that they were not successful in putting her in foal so they tried to back her. By then Flo hated people and argued with everything asked off her, the hatred she felt for these people was like poison and she put up such a fight to get away from them.

They used every gadget on Flo that they could as they tried to break her spirit. The stress of all of this was immense and she turned and put her head into my hands, I felt her emotion in my throat and I cried her tears and apologised for everything mankind had put her through, we stayed like this for a while with Flo absorbing the healing and relaxing.

I had been talking to Joy during the healing and she was amazed at what she was seeing but it answered a lot of questions. It had taken Flo a long time to trust Joy and everything had to be introduced very slowly, if at any time to much was asked of Flo she would withdraw back into herself and Joy could not reach her. Flo had been branded dangerous, Joy was told by her previous owners never to try and ride her. Joy could see beyond the behavior and gave Flo understanding and love and worked at a very slow pace until Flo started trusting again. Two years down the line they are out competing x-country and having a wonderful time together.

Flo holds a lot of her past experiences in her hind quarters which makes her stride shorter than it should be, if Joy was trying to do dressage they would be marked down. Flo has moved on and learnt to trust Joy, I know that held within her pelvis is deep rooted pain and anguish from the past, she was not happy for me to heal the area. I know that the healing energy will go where it is needed, Flo has shared some of her past with us, the rest she has buried and it is her decision if she lets it go. At the moment she has shed enough memories, with Joy's help she has rebuilt her confidence and moved on and they are looking to a future of lots of happy times together.

SOLO

Joy asked me to have a look at Solo her daughter's pony she was worried about him because his behavior had changed and he was refusing to jump which was not like him.

I walked into Solo's stable and introduced myself, straight away I was surprised by how flat he felt, there was no greeting good or bad. There was no interest, I asked him if I could scan his body over and as I did this he stood there quietly and soon started licking and chewing. I straight away picked up heat all along the left hand side of his body, I told Joy what I had found and that due to the energy blocks on the left he would find schooling on the right rein very difficult, he was stiff and could not bend through his body. Joy confirmed that this was happening, his pelvis was also very stiff, as soon as I mentioned this he pulled up his hind leg and asked me to place my hand high up inside which I did, he took a huge amount of healing in this area. Solo told me that he was finding it difficult to jump and to do the work that he needed to do due to an old injury in his pelvis. I told Joy about this and as I carried on healing she confirmed that she would make an appointment to get his back checked.

As I was healing, Solo was doing all the right things, communicating, licking, chewing, yawning but still I was disturbed about the level of his energy. I felt that he should be full of life and cheeky but he wasn't and I asked him about this, straight away I felt a huge loss and emptiness deep within, as if Solo had lost a friend and he wasn't very happy with this. I asked him for more information and he started to lick and chew and yawn as he continued. A new pony had come onto the yard a few weeks ago, since then everything had changed, his friend was paired up with the new pony and Solo was now going out in the field with one of the bigger mares who he really didn't like. The new pony also had his stable and he had been moved to another one. This had upset Solo and was making him very withdrawn and miserable.

I discussed this with Joy and she confirmed that his field and stable had changed; she never thought it would bother him as he seemed to get on with all the horses. Joy agreed to change the stable and field back to how it was before to see if that would make Solo happier.

I left them happy that Solo had been heard and that he would be getting his friend back. I had an email when I got home to say they had moved him back with his friend and already he seemed happier and was back charging around the field like his old self!.

Never underestimate how changes in grazing partners and stables can affect your horse.

LUCIE

I was booked to visit a pony in Axminster, I left home in thick fog not even sure if I would find the stables. The drive took longer than usual and I was pleased to reach my destination and to be greeted by Julie. I was taken to a stable and looked into see a beautiful young pony, straight away I picked up that her energy was low and she needed everyone to be quiet around her. Julie had called me out to see what I could find out about Lucie as she felt there was something she was missing and needed my help.

I entered the stable and after Julie had put the head collar on Lucie I introduced myself. Lucie was not like a youngster who is looking in your pockets and seeing who you are. Lucie just stood there switched off, I felt her over and felt that her body was frail her bones were not strong but she had the deepest and most beautiful soul, the only way I could describe her is like your first teddy bear, always with you comforting and not demanding.

I scanned Lucie over and found heat throughout her body where she had small energy blocks but nothing that would alter her behavior. Then I placed my hands on her neck, here I felt heat radiating out of her. The heat was intense and I kept my hand on the area asking Lucie to accept the healing. As I did this Lucie started to communicate by showing me pictures. She showed me pictures of before she was born inside her mother's womb. She showed me that her neck was bent over in a very peculiar angle and she could not move, this had resulted in a long difficult birth. From what I was seeing it looked like Lucie may have been starved of oxygen during the birth causing the brain to suffer. Whilst I was healing her neck she did a beautiful stretch as the energy cleared and she licked and chewed. Lucie really touched me, the only way I can describe her is as a "special needs" pony, the shortage of oxygen has damaged her brain and so learning is difficult, and this is also why she is so quiet. She is so special and so very lucky to have been with her owner for the past two years, as she has understood her. Julie thought that there was something different but could never put her finger on exactly what.

Julie had given Lucie time to recover because when they rescued her she was very poor; she was malnourished and very frightened. When she reached three and a half Julie thought it was time to start Lucie's education she wanted her to be a lead rein pony for her little girl. They had worked at a slow pace, which gave Lucy time to absorb everything that was asked of her. Had Lucie been in the wrong hands she is the sort of pony who may well have been abused because she is not quick learner. Tougher tactics would have been used and people would have become very angry with her, thinking that she was being naughty when in fact she just couldn't understand. For Lucie to understand, everything has to be black and white and she needs to be given time to absorb what is being asked.

It is the same with horses as humans when things are not quite right and something is different, other senses become stronger, this ponies quietness and companionship that she offers is indescribable.   Julie is pleased that she now knows why Lucie behaves in the way that she does and has decided to keep her as a companion pony to both other horses and people.

JODY

Jody is a beautiful chestnut thoroughbred, his owner Rose wanted to find out how he was feeling as they have been having a few problems. I introduced myself and Jody seemed quite pleased to meet me and accepted my energy. I placed my hand on his right shoulder and found his right side to be very uncomfortable, I could feel huge amounts of heat all through his back where he had energy blocks and this was causing tension and stiffness in his body. I told Rose that at the moment he would find the left rein very difficult as he is full of tension on the right which would prevent him from bending. Rose confirmed that they have been having riding problems and she didn't realise it was because of pain.

As I have explained the heat in the body can be due to experiences in life that have not been dealt with this can be mental and, or, physical trauma.

I started healing Jody and he relaxed and welcomed my help, he was very quick to accept the healing and started licking and chewing and yawning straight away. Rose could not believe how quiet he was, she said that when strangers normally come into the stable Jody becomes very worried and agitated and yet here he was falling asleep. I explained to Rose that he had been waiting for someone to talk to and now was the right time.

I worked down the right side of his body and whilst I was doing this I nearly had to stop. I had the overwhelming feeling in my stomach of panic from being shut in a confined space and feeling very sick. I am not a good traveler and the feeling that I had was the same as when that plane door shuts - horrible. I realised that this would be a feeling that he would have from any small space such as a trailer. Rose confirmed that when she first had him he was a terrible traveler and would shake and sweat, but with gentle driving and travelling him with a horse that is confident he has got a lot better.

As I moved my hands over his body I felt that there was a lot of wear and tear on his bones which has resulted in arthritis. Rose had already told me that Jody had raced, unfortunately, arthritis is an occupational hazard. A lot of race horses are ridden from the age of two and younger and this puts terrible strain on their joints. Their bodies are still growing and the bones are soft it is too much pressure at such a young age.

As I was healing he continued to yawn and lowered his head as the energy shifted. I have been told when treating people who have arthritis that the healing energy warms the joints and brings a welcome release from the nagging pain.

Jody then started to open up, telling me that he had been good at his job. He showed me pictures of a man who had been in his life and the person was Irish it looked like perhaps a groom or jockey as he was very small in his build. I mentioned this to Rose who confirmed that when he was racing he had had a groom who loved him but she didn't know if he was Irish. Later she messaged me to say the jockey who always rode him was Irish. I carried on healing him until his right side was comfortable and Rose told me that there had been a fall that had ended his racing career.

When I went to his left side I knew that this would be different, Jody had some big scars on his shoulder.

As I approached him he became quite agitated and moved away so I kept my hands at a distance until he was happy for me to touch him. I worked down his neck until I was near the scars and then the word "stalls" hit me, he told me "I was young and they started the training to early, it was too much, the stalls were the worst. The space was too small and I panicked wanting to get out" Jody started walking around his stable and I carried on healing him as he explained some more. "I kicked and reared up but the sides kept coming in nothing would move them. But they didn't listen and tied me in the stall but this was even worse I kicked and kicked until the pain of my bruises and cuts became greater than the feeling of no space." Jody took a breath and stood as I placed my hand on his scars and healed the pain caused by this disturbing event.

It seemed that the trainers did listen and instead of using stalls he was in races where they just had to line up before the start. As he was telling me this he yawned and released and his eye became very soft.

I told Rose what Jody had told and shown me and it all started to make sense, the fear of small spaces the difficulties in schooling and the arthritis affecting his movement. Rose then told me how she had come to be with Jody. Rose had visited an animal sanctuary to try a cob, she had been having a break from horses but felt a huge need to be with them again. The horse she tried was lovely and did all that Rose asked, but, there was this other horse calling to her from the field. He didn't take his eyes off her and so she asked about the chestnut in the field. The sanctuary staff told her that he was dangerous and they were thinking of having him put to sleep. Rose asked if she could go and see him and they agreed. As she walked across the field with the horse watching her she felt an intense peace wash over her. As she reached him he nuzzled her and she stroked his face. He looked at her in the eye and she knew that she had to have this horse, everything in her mind said "no" but her heart said yes and she felt that he needed her as much as she needed him.

Rose spoke to the sanctuary staff who were amazed that she

wanted him but they agreed and he was delivered the next day. There started a journey for them both, with time and patience Rose learnt to understand Jody and a relationship was built of trust. There have been problems along the way but they have learnt great lessons together.

Problems had started with Jody becoming older and Rose suddenly wanting to do more in the school. As a result of the healing she realised that Jody could not do the schooling and she made the decision to keep him as her hacking horse.

PIP

I received a call from Alice booking me to see her mare Pip. Pip is an Irish Draught x Cob age seven. Alice took me out to the field explaining along the way that she had owned Pip for six months and she was finding Pip difficult to ride and nobody could get to the bottom of it.

I introduced myself to Pip as Alice put on her head collar and removed her rug. Pip was quite happy for me to get to work and so I gently scanned her over. Straight away a conversation started "It was terrible they didn't know what they were doing". I told Alice this and carried on healing. Pip's body was totally locked on the right hand side the muscles were rigid and schooling would be difficult. These memories of the past were being held in her body causing huge tension and I needed to find out more. I asked Pip if she could tell me more; Pip showed me a rider who sat very heavy in the saddle the person was large and I would say to heavy to be riding Pip. I could see that this person was not an experienced rider and Pip did not feel secure with them. "They did not know what they were doing kick, kick, kick, but if I went forward the reins were tight I had nowhere to go". I felt that at some time Pip would have been schooled, but these people had made her question her ability and confidence. The connection between horse and rider had been all wrong.

Pip showed me pictures of her being lunged relentlessly and so much on the left rein putting great strain on the right hand side of her body being on a continuous circle. Pip again showed me the "heavy" rider and her mouth with the reins really tight and the bit pinching. Pip could not move her neck they would give her no freedom to move properly. Their lack of confidence had turned into fear which was being transferred to Pip.

I told Alice what I had been shown and she confirmed everything that Pip had told me. Since owning Pip, Alice had been quietly working with her and trying to restore her confidence. I carried on working with Pip and she drew my attention to her left side by biting herself there. I placed my hand on the area and straight away I could see the kick of someone's boot in her side. When they had tried to mount Pip she had moved away because she knew being ridden would not be a nice experience, this resulted in the rider kicking her hard from the ground. Bullying tactics, you have hold of the reins and the horse cannot get away from you and the kick from the furious person makes contact. I carried on healing Pip and she licked and chewed and yawned as she relaxed and let the memory go.

Another event that Pip had shown me was that she was an "Old Soul". I sometimes come across horses who have lived here before. Pip had shown me a picture of her pulling an old fashioned cart; the ladies in the cart had white pinafore dresses on and laced up boots. It was a very peaceful and happy life, Pip showed me a young girl who used to come to the field with apples in her pinafore pockets. This was a happy life and Pip finds this life so different, there is no understanding or compassion it is all so different and confusing for her.

Alice is now aware of what Pip has been through and how it has affected her confidence they are working together with guidance, to rebuild Pip's confidence and unlock the schooled horse that is waiting to show herself again.

JACK

Problems come in all shapes and sizes; I was called out by Tara to treat her rescue horse Jack. Jack was a shire x full of feather and very strong, he had the most beautiful big kind eye. Tara had been having problems with Jack, he had come from an animal sanctuary and every time Tara rode Jack he wouldn't do as asked in the school, he refused to leave the yard when hacking and Tara did not know what to do.

When I arrived Jack was tied up outside his stable and I asked if we could take him inside for the treatment. Tara seemed a little anxious but untied him and in we went, by this time a few other people had gathered to watch. I introduced myself to Jack and I could feel the anxiety all around from the people watching, Jack seemed happy for me to be with him so I felt down through his body and scanned him with my eye; I was immediately drawn to his right shoulder. I felt the shoulder and under my hand I felt huge areas of heat. The whole of Jack's side felt blocked, I showed Tara by dowsing over him, when I came to his shoulder the pendulum spiraled violently and when I moved it away it calmed down. It did this over his shoulder down his right fore leg and over both sides of his pelvis. He also had heat in both hocks Tara was amazed and said "that is why I can't school him I thought he was being naughty" the next moment tears were streaming down her face as the anxiety left her body now that she finally understood.

I started healing Jack's shoulder, although Jack is a big horse inside he is small and vulnerable and lacking in confidence. Jack became quiet and still as I worked over his body, at times his breathing became very heavy and my chest was tight with his anxiety, I worked on releasing this until the feeling left my chest. I moved to his pelvis and was told by my guides that there was a lot of wear and tear resulting in the joints not working properly. I sent healing to the area until the heat calmed down and Jack was licking and chewing and yawning.

I then moved back to his shoulder it felt like there was a red hot poker down the length of his shoulder and the pain from it went down his leg. Whilst I was healing the area Jack showed me pictures of him in a driving harness, he was working with another horse. They were not pulling a cart and the ground they were walking on was very rough. Then I saw it, they were working a plough, Jack then showed me pictures of him stumbling and falling on this leg and he smashed his shoulder against the other horses harness. This was where the damage was done the heat and discomfort is from an old injury.

I told Tara what I had seen and how he had injured his shoulder and she confirmed that he had been on a farm and was used to work the land until the farmer had lost his farm and taken the two horses to the sanctuary.

I carried on healing Jack, he told me he hated being on his own, he had always been with the other horse who gave him confidence, Tara confirmed that when they arrived at the sanctuary the other horse had been ill and put to sleep. Nobody had thought to tell Jack what had happened to his friend and I broke the news to him. He licked and chewed as he absorbed the information.

Tara loved Jack to bits but could never understand why there were communication blocks between them when she rode him. I explained to Tara that Jack had spent his life going in straight lines, he had not been schooled, and as he was now well into his teens it was a little late to start. Straight lines he and his body could cope with and long gentle plods but this would be all.

Jack's lack of confidence being ridden out on his own was also because he had always been worked as a pair. Jack showed me pictures of a hilly area and a man leading the other horse and Jack following on behind. It was his daily routine, the man caught the other horse and Jack knew that he then followed them into the barn. He had not been led or had to do anything on his own, he doesn't understand how to walk with you on a lead rope, walk in front and he would follow. Tara was amazed because this is how Jack is, when she first got him she tried to lead Jack to the field but found it impossible. But if another horse went to the field at the same time in front of him he followed on behind.

Everything began to make sense to Tara, as I carried on healing Jack she relaxed and let the tears fall. She had been so frustrated and had no understanding of Jack's behavior until now. Because she did not understand she and other people at the yard thought that Jack was being ill mannered and rude so whenever anyone went to do anything with him they expected the worst. Their own energy would be filled with anxiety and Jack would not want to be with them. If they forced the issue he would panic resulting in people being trod on and crushed in the stable. Now I understood the anxiety when I asked for Jack to be put in his stable. Tara now has decisions to make, Jack will never be able to do the schooling and hacking that Tara wants to do so important choices have to be made.

I left Tara and in the coming days she phoned me to say that it was a very hard decision but she had decided to send Jack back to the sanctuary. On his arrival I went and treated him to help him with the change, I am happy to say that he will spend the rest of his life there and he seems very happy with the decision.

JO

I had been asked to visit Jo by his owner Donna, I knew no other information and felt from my phone conversation with Donna that this could be a difficult appointment.

When I arrived at the yard Jo was in his stable, I introduced myself to Donna, she seemed quite withdrawn and did not want to talk and so I got to work. I introduced myself to Jo and asked if I could help him. As normal I placed my hand on his shoulder letting him get used to my energy and then I scanned his body.

I felt pain over his body, his back and shoulders were tense and I asked Donna if she was riding him because I felt that he needed checking by a vet or a physio. Donna confirmed that they were not working at the moment. I started healing down through his back and Donna stood to the side of the stable, I heard the word "RESTRICTED" in my mind in big letters. He showed me a picture of him and Donna in a school, "I couldn't find my stride the reins were too tight" the school had show jumps in it and I asked Donna if they did a lot of schooling. She replied that they did not have a school at the yard but they had good hacking. I was confused he was shouting restricted at me and showing me pictures of them in a school but Donna said they didn't have a school.

I asked him if he was sure, he shouted the word even louder. I carried on healing him and he licked and chewed and yawned letting the stress of the situation go and I carried on down his body beginning to doubt my ability that day. He then told me that they were mirroring each other and that things had changed in her life. I asked Donna if anything had recently changed in her own life and she replied "no". Jo was very worried about Donna but it really was like talking to a brick wall, her energy was really low, and I realised that I was obviously on a test and failing this horse miserably. I carried on healing the horse and I could feel the spasms in his back releasing.

I carried on healing him and he relaxed in his body and mind and licked and chewed releasing the anxiety with huge yawns. I worked my way all down through his body and was very worried about how battered it seemed. I could get no more information out of his owner and so carried on giving him love and healing until he was totally relaxed with his nose nearly on the floor.

After the session his owner began to talk to me, she told me that they had recently had a terrible fall jumping in a school and she had been airlifted to hospital. Immediately the words restricted and couldn't find my stride made more sense to me, if only his owner had opened up we could have gone a lot deeper with Jo. I asked her about her injuries, she had a damaged shoulder and bruised ribs, he said he was mirroring her, his pain was the same and more. After a little while she then told me that she had also lost her job the week before – huge change in her life.
Sometimes people set you up to be tested, his owner wanted to know if I would tell her about the fall, that isn't how this horse processed the event, he was in the moment not thinking about the fall but worried about how his owner felt in her body and mind. He told me how it had happened he was restricted in his stride, after talking to Donna it seems he did not take off correctly resulting in them both falling to the ground.

PETRA

I was called to see Petra because Sue her young owner wanted to try and find out a little more about the mare. When she had got her Petra could not be ridden or touched and was in a very sad and stressed place. Sue has done very well, taking her time and learning to understand Petra .

When I arrived at the yard Petra was out in the field Sue went out to get her, Petra came in at a great rate of knots with Sue in hot pursuit. Sue managed to catch Petra and we took her into the stable. Petra did not want me very close to her so I kept my distance and sent healing to her, whilst talking to her all the time. I slowed my breathing so that my energy was as small as possible and I kept my head low. Petra was pacing on the spot and did not want me anywhere near her. This is quite common in horses that have had to cope with a lot of mental and physical abuse. They are on red alert and pick up on my energy straight away, I told her that we would work at her speed and we would deal with one issue at a time and if she didn't want to talk that was fine but I asked her to accept the healing to help her relax.

After a while Petra allowed me to move closer, once I was close enough I reached out a hand towards her shoulder and her skin started twitching as she felt the energy. For a moment this scared Petra and I reassured her that I would not hurt her, I slowly scanned her body. There were huge areas of heat some from stored emotions not let go, some from physical abuse which injured her. Poor Petra had been through an awful lot and she didn't want to talk but was quite happy for me to heal her body, this can happen with some horses that have been abused. A bit like people, they don't want to talk, they just need healing and help working out how to move forward. She has learnt to live in the moment again realising that she has a wonderful lovely caring owner and everything she could possibly need. For Petra to start talking about the past the moment would be gone and the past would be back, so we worked on releasing all the energy blocks in her body so that her energy could flow and heal the old wounds. The release came in lots of yawns and licking and chewing, Sue wanted to know why Petra could not cope with being schooled, it was really holding them back. I felt from Petra that she has a huge fear of getting things wrong, in the past she has been beaten for not understanding. Now when the rules change and something is asked of her that she does not understand she panics, which puts her in flight mode and stops her. Sue needs to take each step very slowly to try and keep Petra in a calm place so that she can keep thinking and concentrating on the task in hand and not panic about what could happen if she gets it wrong.

When a horse as sensitive as Petra has been abused it takes a lot of time to repair the damage, if it can ever be repaired. Years of being misunderstood and made to feel useless and being beaten can take a long time to get over. But with a good home and an understanding owner and lots of time and patience anything is possible.

At the end of the session Petra was in a lovely place incredibly relaxed and stress free. Letting go of the negative energy will also heal the tension in her body, which was resulting in muscle aches and pains.

ZARA

Zara is a beautiful 17.3hh 5year old German Warmblood, she will not fully mature in body and mind until she is about 8 years old, please remember this when you read her story.

I was called to visit Zara by Nicky the yard manager where Zara is kept on full livery, Nicky did not know what to do with Zara so I booked her in for that week and drove to the yard. Zara was kept on a dressage training yard, I do not often get called into professional yards and as I drove there I knew I would have to be strong as I would not like all that I saw.

I found the yard and pulled into the car park which was in the middle of the stables, everywhere I looked horses were staring at me. As I got out of the car all the horses started fidgeting and calling me, I sent them all love and healing and told them I had only come to see one horse. I find it very hard to turn away from horses but unless I have been booked to treat a horse I cannot treat them, all I can do is send love and healing to them.

Nicky came over and introduced herself and took me to Zara's stable, as we approached the stable I immediately noticed the hay net tied up outside the stable. As we got near the stable door Zara's head came over with her ears back and teeth bared ready to bite us. From seeing this I realised that the people on the yard were scared of Zara. Nicky asked me what I needed and I asked her to put a head collar and rope on Zara and remove her rug. Nicky took a big breath and entered the stable, straight away Zara put her ears back and as Nicky was putting the headcollar on tried to bite her many times. I had not seen such an angry horse for a very long time, I entered the stable, and the fear coming from Zara made me feel sick. I put out my hand to Zara and she instantly went to bite it, I kept my hand there and spoke to Zara as I started healing her at a distance. I could smell her fear, every muscle was ready to be used and her senses were all over the place.

I communicated to Zara that I was not going to hurt her and that I wanted to help her. The whole time Zara was on red alert, her skin was tight; if she could have she would have galloped far away. But Zara could not let her flight response take over, Nicky had hold of her and the door was closed. So all she could do was stand and attack. It was obvious to me that something very bad had happened to Zara to make her this way.

I was not getting anywhere healing from a distance, so I placed my hand on her head collar and the other hand on her shoulder. I was keeping my energy low and I told Nicky how to breathe to bring her energy down, I then had a window when Zara calmed slightly and I could communicate with her. "There is too much pressure, can't cope can't cope, all too quick, when I get it wrong they punish me, the whips the spurs the beatings, so I fight back." Zara showed me images of the beatings, one was someone hitting her around the head with their fists.

This poor mare had taken so much and had been forced to fight back, the flight mechanism would not help her they had hold of her and so she stood her ground and fought back. The only problem with this is that anger fuels anger. A thump makes Zara bite so the human thumps harder and so it goes on in
a never ending vicious circle. What needs to happen is for the person to take a step back and think about what is happening.

Zara is a baby, her mind and body cannot cope with the pressure. Zara is a tall beautiful horse with presence, but she has been ambushed by mankind. She needs to be allowed to be a youngster to relax and grow and with that will come maturity of mind. Zara is not so different from a teenager, over load them with pressure and bully them and they will blow and become angry and violent exactly the same as Zara.

I started working with Zara using body energy in a way another horse would, no violence or words just body energy. By doing this I enabled her to relax enough for me to offer healing, but the moments were short, her insecurity soon took over and the teeth would start biting. Once she caught me on my arm and drew blood, instantly she expected to be hit, instead I told her I understood and carried on healing breaking the vicious circle of anger if only for a short while. I carried on healing Zara for as long as she could relax which were short periods of time, my heart cried for her and I sent all my love and healing to her.

I turned to Nicky and told her what Zara had said and explained that the pressure needs to come off. I told her that Zara needs to be turned away for a year and then to start again but in a gentle way that Zara would understand. Nicky said that could not happen, Zara had been brought by her owner as a dressage horse and she expected her to be schooled so that she could compete her. Nicky then told me that Zara has had four owners already and has been moved from many yards. I told Nicky that it had to stop Zara could not cope and if they carried on I could see Zara having to be destroyed as she would become too dangerous to handle.

I gave all my love to Zara and left the yard my tears of frustration falling, I knew the appointment on a professional yard would be hard but it was more than that, as I drove away I don't think I have ever felt so disillusioned with mankind. Why can't people see what they are doing? Why do they not feel it in their heart?

Why are they led so much by ego that nothing else matters? Things need to change……….

ARNIE

I get called out to many "problem horses" some of them are a result of what people have done to them and some are a complete surprise……………………….

One surprise was Arnie, his owner Gemma emailed me because she didn't know what to do with Arnie, he would not go out into the field and was very jumpy with loud noises. As I drove to Gemma's I thought about the horse that I was booked to see, I knew that Arnie had come over from Germany as a youngster. I know that in Germany the horses are not turned out very much and wondered it this would be the cause of his problem.

As I walked down the garden path with Gemma a big beautiful head looked over the stable door and said "you came then". Some horses are like this and talk to me straight away, Gemma put on Arnie's head collar and I introduced myself to Arnie. As I scanned him over I could feel huge tension in his shoulders and he was quite agitated, he needed to talk and yet at the same time there was an element of fear. He stood snatching at his hay as I told Gemma what I had felt in his shoulders, I explained to Arnie that Gemma was worried about him because he would not go outside to graze and I was here to help him.

I placed my hand on Arnie's shoulder and he told me that he had been waiting for me, straight away he started showing me pictures, it was as if I was watching a film. It was of a war, I soon realised that Arnie was an old soul meaning he had been on this earth before and what I was being shown was of his past life. I asked Arnie why he had come back he replied "to tell my story" this is Arnie's story:

Arnie started walking around his stable he had waited a long time to see me and now he was full of emotion and tension, it was too much to stand still so I walked with him with my hand on his shoulder. "We shouldn't have been there it wasn't safe," he showed me the battle field and the horses with the soldiers marching, they were all in a long line I could feel the fear, there seemed to be hundreds of them. As they marched forward the cannon's fired and the noise was deafening. The air was filled with smoke, bullets and shrapnel. "We could do nothing we should not have been there" I felt his nerves in my stomach and my mouth became dry. Arnie was now pulling me around as I worked with him, from what Arnie was showing me I think he would have been the senior officer's horse. The guns were going off all around them and the horses were falling one after the other. Screams could be heard from both horse and man as they lay their dying. Arnie started biting at his side and I placed my hand on the area and directed healing energy into him as he continued.

"It went on and on all the horses around me were dead, the field was green but littered with bodies." Arnie showed me pictures of the Cannons and soldiers but I could not make out the uniforms.

Words cannot describe what I was being shown the message from it was that they should not have been there. The battle that Arnie had taken me through was like nothing I had ever experienced before, the whole time I was with Arnie we were circling his box and he was trying to bite me as he released his anger. When he had finished showing me this part of his life he stood still and accepted the healing he so very desperately needed, he was very hot and exhausted. At one point I thought he was going to lie down but he wobbled and then stretched from head to tail. He then yawned and yawned as the memories were released and relaxation took over. After a while he came to and walked to the door with me, we looked at the green field, I saw it as a place for him to graze and play with his friends. He saw it as a field of death and he feared not only for his safety but also the safety of the other horses with him. Just proves that nothing is as straight forward as you first think.

I carefully explained everything to Gemma who at one time had become quite worried; it was totally out of character for Arnie to bite people. I told her it was part of the healing, it was his way of releasing the emotion of anger that he felt about the situation. I explained everything that I had seen and that Arnie saw green fields as a place of death and war. I asked to return in two weeks to carry out another healing with Arnie to help him.

I returned two weeks later to treat Arnie again, the first appointment had explained why he did not like going out but has not helped him to overcome his fears. So I knew that I had to do a different healing with him today and I asked my guides for help. He was pleased to see me, I started healing him but told him that we needed to stay in this life. He instantly relaxed and the communication started to flow, this time he showed me pictures of when he was young with his mum and then being kept in a barn with other youngsters. As he was showing me his life I healed his body and he stayed deeply relaxed, he showed me his life in Germany where he didn't go out, you were worked and then spent your time in the stable. It was only when he came to England that people started putting him out in fields.

I asked Arnie to come on a journey with me and he agreed, I kept my hands on him and can only describe what happened next as a joint meditation. As we breathed deeply together I took Arnie to his gate and we looked out at the green field, I straight away felt his anxiety and told him it was ok and to take a good look around. See the trees and the sky and hear the birds singing, there were no guns or wars to fight. In our meditation I walked into the field and asked Arnie to join me, he hesitated and then took the few strides to join me. I told him to smell the air there were no smells of gun powder and death only sweet summer grass. I encouraged Arnie to graze and he did staying relaxed. I then carried on healing Arnie and brought him back into the stable, he licked and chewed and yawned and remained very relaxed. I then told Arnie that when Gemma took him into the field he needed to remember what we had just done, to take a big breath and to stay relaxed. Very slowly Arnie came out of the meditation and went and put his head in Gemma's hands.

I explained to Gemma what I had done and asked her to leave his stable door open and the gate to the field. They are lucky that they keep Arnie and his friends at home so this is not a problem, by doing this Arnie can walk out into the field but know that he can always go inside if he becomes nervous.

The second healing was completely different to the first much more relaxed and I left knowing that Arnie was in a much better place in his mind than when I first met him.

LOUIS

I received a phone call from a lady called Jackie requesting an urgent appointment for her horse Louis. I was having a quiet week, so two days later I drove to Berkshire to meet Jackie and Louis. Louis was a 5 year old German Warm blood gelding and he had been brought over from abroad, judging by my conversation with Jackie things were not going too well.

I arrived to find Jackie a bag of nerves and quite emotional, she kept saying that she didn't know what he would be like with me, I told her not to worry. Jackie led me down the drive to the horses that were in their stables, one stable door had a very friendly head greeting us, the other, a bottom with legs attached ready to kick. I asked Jackie to put a head collar on Louis she disappeared round the back of the stables and came in through a back door so that she could catch him, she did not trust him not to kick out if she walked in through the front stable door. I watched all of this with interest and entered the stable; I could feel Louis's anger and

Jackie's nerves rebounding off each other. I took hold of the rope and asked Jackie to stand to the side of the stable. I let Louis sniff my hands but all he wanted to do was bite and show me in no uncertain terms how he felt. I knew I had to help Louis and undid his rug, whilst doing this Louis was biting the air he was very stressed and angry.

I moved away from him and watched him for a while and quietly sent healing to him, I then asked Louis if he would let me help him and placed a hand on his shoulder. Louis started walking round the stable I asked Jackie to go outside the stable so that I knew she was safe and I concentrated 100% on Louis. I felt that I needed to bring his energy down; I kept my energy low and started to move his body around the stable, directing his hindquarters away from me with my body energy like another horse would. After a while he sniffed my hand and talking to him quietly he let me place it on his shoulder. His body was tense and solid the skin didn't move, it was like touching lead, he sniffed my hand again and then very slowly started licking and sucking my fingers. Whilst he was doing this I communicated with him that I was not going to hurt him I was there to help.

I slowly scanned his body with my hand and found the left side was completely blocked with stress and anger which he showed with lots of attempts to bite me. He suddenly became very still and quiet and his eyelids relaxed. He then started to share his story; he took me to a barn, he said he had been left tied up in there for hours. He showed me people trying to come near him but he would not let them near him he was scared, he lashed out with teeth and legs to keep them away. This worked but he was left for a very long time with no feed or water. He then went onto show me a time with his mum when life had been good; it seems from the time when he had been weaned his life became totally different. I carried on healing his left side, as I was healing he drew my hand to different parts of his side and everywhere I placed my hand I could see and feel the beatings that he had had, every thump and kick. I could see that he had learnt to fight back and at one time the scene was indescribable, he showed me the anger coming from the man. The kicks and thumps as the man in a blind fury attacked him. As he was showing me this he was barging me out of the way and stamping his feet and biting to show all his emotions within.

Louis had spent a long time angry and I knew that I was not going to reach him with healing alone; before I had to leave I wanted this poor boy to relax. So I asked for guidance, I knew that any sort of dominant behavior would send him into a rage so I had to work very gently and slowly, even the shake of the rope sent him into a rage. If anyone had tried to teach Louis a lesson or put him in a roundpen his anger would have tipped him over the edge. I carried on working him slowly on the rope, using body energy and healing, eventually he calmed down and started to lick and chew.

After what seemed like forever Louis completely relaxed and I asked Jackie to take a big breath and to come and try working him on the rope with her energy. I explained what she had to do and that this was a way that she could always calm Louis down.

I then carried on healing Louis until he was yawning releasing all the stress out of his body his eye was soft and his body relaxed. While Louis was snoozing Jackie told me his story, Jackie already owned a Warm Blood and decided after the death of her pony to buy another. She contacted her horse's breeder and told them what she was looking for, they arranged for her to travel abroad and view the horses. She saw Louis lunged, as he had not yet been backed, had him vetted and then arranged for him to go to full livery to be backed whilst she arranged for him to be brought to the UK.

Jackie returned eight weeks later, she went to see him being loaded for his journey home to the UK. She said that she will never forget the sight that greeted her; the horse in front of her looked nothing like the one she had bought two months earlier. He was trying to attack everyone; he was thin and obviously very angry. Jackie knew something had happened and did some investigating, it seemed that the girlfriend of the rider who was backing Louis had decided to ride him and Louis had thrown her off badly hurting her. The trainer had decided to beat Louis and the beating had lasted a long time, he left him tied up for hours and he took all of his aggression out on Louis. This resulted in Louis coming to the UK as a very unhappy horse.

Jackie had tried love and understanding and had also paid for the help of different trainers but no one could reach him this is why she had called me. I left Jackie and Louis a lot happier than when I had arrived but I said to Jackie that if she could not cope with Louis she could not sell him as he would be dangerous in the wrong hands. She had already realised this and said that she had decided that if this didn't work she would have him put to sleep.

The next evening I received a phone call from Jackie, I was dreading her news, she told me that the man who helped her with her horses in the mornings had phoned her to ask whether Louis had been doped. She asked why and he told her that for the first time Louis had been pleased to see him and he had been an angel to take out and bring in!! I was so pleased, the healing had enabled Louis to talk about what had happened to him to let the emotions go and rebalance his energy, and it seemed that he was now in a much better place and happy, resulting in a much kinder horse. Jackie is training Louis herself, they are forming a fantastic partnership and enjoying each other's company. Both are relaxed and happy.

BLUE

I drove out to the beautiful New Forest to meet a lady called Sally and her horse Blue, all I knew about Blue was that he could be unpredictable.

I arrived and met a very nervous Sally, as we walked to the field I kept on talking to Sally to try and get her to relax. I asked Sally to put Blue's headcoller on and to remove his rug, she hesitated took a breath and walked up to Blue. Straight away he picked up on Sally's anxiety and was difficult to catch and would not stand still for her. I realised that something had gone very wrong with this relationship and I needed to get to the bottom of it.

I walked over to Blue and introduced myself and his reply was to try and dominate me by pushing me around. I started scanning Blue over and he started to communicate with me straight away. Telling me that he wanted Sally to spend more time with him and to be more confident "she makes me nervous" he said. As he was talking to me he was trying to bite Sally and barging into her, so I was not at all surprised that she spent as little time with him as possible and when she did go to him she was very nervous. I took hold of the rope as his behavior really was not acceptable and he was now directing his anger at me. I carried on sending healing to him and left the communication link open, he was becoming more and more agitated. From what he was showing me from his early life he had always been firmly controlled by men. There were no grey areas just black and white, the men told him what to do and he did it or they would hit him until he did. These were rules that he understood, since being sold Blue had found life very confusing there was nobody to tell him what to do so he had become the dominant one and this had resulted in him being sold many times. Sally had been trying to show him love and understanding, this was a language Blue did not understand it was a "grey" area and grey area's brought out the worst in him. Someone had to be in control and if the person wasn't tough enough for the job then Blue would be the dominant partner.

He was becoming very pushy with me so I worked him on the rope; he did not like this at all and reared up at me, with my energy I reared up on him. This completely shocked him, his energy came down and he licked and chewed as he realised that not only does this women talk his language but that it is someone who can take control and make the decisions. I carried on healing through his body and explained to Sally what had been going on. Blue had been the dominant one in their partnership and this needed to change, I explained to Sally what I had been doing and how she could control her body energy in the same way to become someone that Blue listened to. Sally was keen to have a go so I passed her the rope.

Straight away Blue sensed the weaker energy and took control, I again took the rope back explaining what I was doing and Blue stood quietly, at the end half asleep and secure. I told Sally we needed to practice on the energy work and made an appointment the following week to go back out.

At the second appointment I could see a big change Sally was in control and relaxed, she had been working with Blue on the rope and their relationship was improving. I started working with Blue and he remembered everything that we had done the previous week. I worked him a bit harder and found that if I went to quick he became angry so we slowed everything down so that he understood and was happy. I explained to Sally that they needed to work slowly; Blue needed a chance to understand what was being asked of him. Like people are all different so are horses, Blue's brain needed time to process new instructions where as other horses could work quicker, they are all different and should be treated as individuals what works for one may not work for another.

It is wonderful when through my work horses are understood and the relationship between horse and owner completely changes for the better. If both parties understand then the joint goal becomes achievable.

HARRY

Harry is a lovely chestnut TB his owner Jill had called me as she was worried about him, nobody can find anything wrong with him but she felt he wasn't right.

I walked into Harry's stable to be greeted by a kind and gentle eye, you can find out a lot about a horse by looking at the eye, some say it is the window to the soul. I introduced myself to Harry and scanned both sides of his body; the difference between right and left was amazing. On the right from his head to his tail he was stiff in his body where he was holding emotional issues. This would make schooling on the left rein very difficult and Jill confirmed that it was impossible; however, the left side was supple and relaxed. I dowsed over both sides so that Jill could see the difference, on the left it was quiet but on the right it spiraled.

I then set to work, I asked Harry if I could help him, at first he thought it was a great game and it took a bit of persuading to get Harry to concentrate. But when he did let me in and I started healing the right side the communication came through. He put his head down and sniffed my black riding boots and then Jill's boots and fine chaps. He told me about a man who had worn what Jill was wearing, boots and chaps. Harry did not like this man, Harry showed me a picture of the man riding him, Harry was doing all that he could to get him off even running down the side of a wall to force him off. It didn't work and Harry had a hard beating to teach him a lesson. I could see that he had been hit around the head and Jill confirmed that he had been very head shy. Harry then sniffed my boots which are heavier than Jill's and he showed me a much larger man who he had been scared of, the man used to kick him in the stomach and thump him at the same time, when Harry pulled away he would pull hard on the reins from the ground damaging Harry's mouth. By now Jill was quite emotional and she told me that Harry had been put into a racing yard and she knew something had happened but didn't know what. She recognised the description Harry gave of the men the bigger one was the yard owner and the other was the jockey.

I carried on working down Harry's body releasing all the pent up emotions which had made his body rigid and caused him to be lame. He would either become very stressed as he was releasing the emotion or very relaxed and this went on for about an hour. After his right side became soft and I could touch him without a violent reaction he was so lovely, giving me lots of cuddles and nuzzling my face. The difference between the sides of his body was extreme the right was like a bright red poker going right the way down his body and the left a piece of string. I felt that Harry needed the help of a good physio and left Jill with a phone number.

I visited Harry again a few weeks later; the physio had been twice and manipulated his back and pelvis. Healing is wonderful for releasing stored emotions within the body but where things need putting back in and realigning then a qualified physio needs to be called. This time Harry was much more comfortable and happy he had a sense of humour and was quite cheeky. He then became serious and told me about Jill and how stressed she was and this upset him. I mentioned this to Jill who burst into tears and off loaded some of her problems, whilst she was doing this Harry licked and chewed as he released her tension. Harry wants Jill to spend time with him relaxing, when she is stressed and upset go and cry with him, horses are amazing healers and can make us feel so much better. He also wanted them both to go for quiet rides, this would do his body good to be stretched and it would also be relaxing for Jill.

At the end of the healing Harry was very relaxed and yawned and yawned, Jill was also feeling exhausted from letting her tears flow.

If you ever have a feeling that your horse is not being treated well by others please listen to your inner voice and do something about it.

LILLY

Lilly's owner and I have been trying to get a date together for ages and at last the universe decided now was the time. I arrived at a beautiful yard horses and foals all grazing by a beautiful lake! Lilly is kept on livery at the yard and her owner Sue was there to welcome me.

Lilly is an Irish Draught, 18 years old and has been with Sue for 9 months. Sue had called me because she wanted to know that Lilly was happy and wanted to see if there was anyway that they could improve their relationship; she said that Lilly could be a little aloof and headstrong in hand. We took Lilly into the school where it was quiet and I explained to Sue what I would do, I began to scan Lilly with my eye and hand. I found tension in the shoulders and pelvis which would make Lilly stiff.

The first thing Lilly said to me was that she had had a foal, there was a lot of anger in this statement and I asked her if she would like to talk about it some more. She then showed me a picture of the foal on the ground it was dead and didn't look like it had gone full term. Lilly was very angry that she had not been aloud to touch the foal it had just been taken away and she was left to get on with it. While she was telling me this I was directing healing into her shoulder where all the anxiety was held. Lilly then showed me more pictures. Lilly was being held by a large man and there was anger and anxiety in the air. Two more men were with a stallion and they were trying to get the stallion to mount her. Lilly was full of anger and there was no way that she wanted this to happen. She bit and kicked out doing everything in her power to stop what was happening

As I was treating Lilly Sue was crying Lilly's tears she could not believe how emotional she was feeling I told her to let the tears

fall. As she did this Lilly was yawning and releasing all the pent up anger that she
had been holding in her body. Lilly has a problem with people touching her back legs and this is due to the treatment she received during this time. They had used hobbles on her hind legs to stop her kicking out at the stallion but that did not work there was no way she was going to be violated.

Lilly had spent her life being picked up and put down, not just the once but many times, she could be quite dominant in her manners and tended to put people off. Her first experiences with mankind had not been good and along with the anger that she held inside about the experience and the loss of her foal she had worked out a way to keep people away from her.

 I carried on healing Lilly and her story moved to when she was younger, she showed me pictures of her being hunted, but it wasn't English hunting. They were using big dogs the size and build of a greyhound with a curly coat, this was quite early on in her life. The hunting was hard and she had had a fall and damaged her right shoulder which I directed healing into. I felt very strongly that Lilly had chosen Sue and I mentioned this to her. Sue confirmed that she was a novice horse owner and when looking for a horse she had seen a photo of Lilly and knew that she had to see her. Everyone had thought her mad as the photo wasn't the best shot and Lilly was a four hour drive away. But, Sue would not be put off, something was pulling her to Lilly, she rode her and paid for her knowing that Lilly was meant to be with her. She paid for a lorry to collect her and it took 4 hours to load Lilly! This was not perhaps the best start. Some would have walked away but the pull for Lilly was so strong Sue was determined to get her home. Sue has spent the first 9 months getting through the
winter and building a relationship with Lilly, now that spring was here they could start exploring the beautiful New Forest which is on their doorstep.

Lilly is going to have a wonderful life in the New Forest going for gentle hacks, which is great because of the shoulder injury she would find it very difficult to school. Before Lilly drifted off into a lovely healing doze Sue and I spoke about the difficulties she has been having with catching and leading Lilly. Sue read on my website about trying to catch a horse that doesn't want to know, and how it is best to back off and concentrate on your breathing so that you become grounded and think of Lilly coming towards you. Sue had tried this and found catching Lilly much easier, Sue now realises that if she is in a hurry or had a bad day there is no way that Lilly will be caught. She picks up on the high energy as soon as Sue approaches the field, so Sue was overcoming the problem of catching Lilly but wanted advice on leading Lilly because she was very head strong, if she did not want to walk on she wouldn't. If she wanted grass she would take Sue to it! I explained to Sue about using energy to direct Lilly the same way as another horse would.

Other people at the yard had told Sue to use a stick but this was not something that she wanted to do she wanted to find another way. So I taught Sue how to direct energy from her body towards Lilly's like another horse would. Lilly must keep her head with Sue all the time so that she has control of Lilly and they can both be safe. I showed Sue how to ask Lilly to turn by using her body energy, her head stays with you and her bottom moves away. Sue tried this and was amazed how easy it was to direct Lilly's body and this could be done if she refused to walk on and if Lilly started leading Sue. I left Sue very happy with the outcome of our time together and when I got home there was an email waiting for me:

"Thank you so much for the session with Lilly today, I could certainly tell she was relaxed!!It was really interesting to hear about her past and to learn how I can strengthen the bond I have with her. It's so reassuring to know that I am doing the right things with her - I can't thank you enough."

MEGAN

Megan is a mare of a client who had been on box rest for a month. The vets have treated her, she had a huge fluid filled lump on her leg but was not lame. There seemed to be confusion over the cause of the lump and Jo her owner asked if I could come and have a chat with Megan to see if we could get any answers. I have visited Jo's other horse before but this was my first session with Megan.

I arrived to find Megan in her stable waiting for me, I spoke to her and she was quite happy for me to enter the stable which I was told is unusual some people have to go in armed with a broom! I introduced myself to Megan who seemed very pleased to see me and stood while I scanned her over. I felt huge energy blocks in her pelvis; I also felt in my own body that the drainage of the body was not working properly. As a result of this her joints felt stiff and uncomfortable. Jo confirmed that Megan had become quite stiff over recent months. I felt that magnetic boots could help Megan and asked Jo if she would look into them.

Whilst I was scanning Megan she opened the conversation and was very chatty "I have her attention now, usually it is always the other one, and I never get a look in any more, never rides me it's always him!" Him is Jo's other horse who had recently joined the herd and as he is a rescue has needed a lot of Jo's attention. Whilst Megan was talking she was showing signs of stress and anger, I asked her to breathe deeply and calm down before we carried on. "I always looked after her, taught her everything and now I am second best" I told Jo what Megan was saying and she laughed and said that everything Megan was saying was true. Jo and Megan had been together for years, Megan had been her only horse until recent months when Jo had brought a gelding to ride as she felt Megan was now ready to retire.

I carried on working with Megan and placed my hand over the swelling on her hind leg, as I was doing this she took my attention to the wall and showed me a picture of her hurting herself on the wall. It actually felt like Megan had done it on purpose to get Jo's attention. I thought about this for a moment and decided that I needed to pass the information on. I said, "I know it sounds silly but from what Megan is showing me she hurts herself to get your attention and has done it before". Jo thought about this for a moment and we talked about some of the other injuries that Megan had sustained over the years and a pattern started to form. Whenever Megan had to share Jo she injured herself in some way so that she got the attention back!

I told Jo that Megan wanted her to ride her again, as far as she was concerned she was not ready to retire. Jo said that she had stopped riding Megan because of her hoof problems and her age but she has agreed to perhaps take her into the school for a play. I told Megan this and she said that would be good as long as she was ridden before him!

Megan then relaxed and I carried on with the healing, all of a sudden Megan turned her head to Jo's Mum who was standing outside the stable "I don't like her" she said. I tried to keep this to myself but Megan started to stamp her front leg on the ground so I took a big breath and told Jo and her Mum. They both burst out laughing; Jo's mum already knew this as Megan had made her feelings known many times. It appears that Megan is jealous of Jo's relationship with the new horse and her Mum!

Megan is a very beautiful mare and a strong character which has caused problems in the past. Jo has had to learn to ride the way that is acceptable to Megan and she has taught her an awful lot. For some people a strong willed mare is too much and they are put up for sale quite quickly but it seems Jo and Megan reached an understanding many years ago and they have had many good years together.

COLO

My work takes me all over the country; I had been booked to visit a horse called Colo who was lucky enough to be kept on a yard next to the beach. Amie has owned Colo for 6 years and the years have not been easy, she bought Colo when she was two years old and their journey together has been unusual to say the least.

On meeting Colo I watched as Amie put on her head collar and removed her rug it was obvious that she was a very nervous horse. She started licking and chewing straight away, like a lot of horses they become quite anxious when they meet me, must seem strange to them they see a human and yet I speak horse. For one who is as anxious as Colo this can be too much, so I took my time talking to her and introducing myself. When Colo had taken a breath and relaxed I gently stroked my hand all over her body, her skin was tight and stressed, her muscles were rigid. I needed to reassure Colo that everything would be ok so that I could try and get her to relax. Colo had energy blocks in her neck and back I realised that I had to work slowly if I was going to help her.

I started offering healing to Colo who found it difficult to concentrate; she stayed very close to Amie. She kept on nudging Amie with her nose she touched her neck and then down her legs telling me that Amie had pain. I asked Amie if she suffered with neck pain and pain in her legs and she smiled and said she did ever since her fall from Colo. Colo was very sorry and did not mean to hurt Amie but she could not cope, Amie explained that Colo had been quite agitated the day of the fall and looking back she should not have ridden her. Due to life being very busy Colo had had time off and Amie had been in a hurry which for Colo was too much, resulting in Amie being bucked off and being air lifted to hospital.

As I was healing Colo I had my guide talking to me - all of my work, I do with the help of spirit guides; my main guide when I am working with the horses is Franko who is Italian and full of energy. I have a team of spirit guides who work through me helping the horses that we meet.

As I was working Franko became quite agitated and said that it was due to interbreeding too much messing around with Mother Nature people always trying to get better. He became very concerned as this is something that we are seeing more and more of. The breeding programs that people set up to breed the best horses are breeding horses with disabilities there is "to much meddling it should be left to Mother Nature "he said.

As I was healing Colo the messages I was being given was that Colo has trouble understanding what is being asked of her. The signals are not clear to Colo's brain she is slow to understand and if she was a person she would be described as having learning difficulties. Because of this she becomes very anxious and then the resulting emotion is anger due to frustration. The problem Amie has been having with her horse is because she needs everything to be very slowly explained, she needs time to understand. This was demonstrated when I worked her on the rope, as long as I gave her time for the message to reach the brain, then the message to reach the legs it was like a light bulb moment. There was understanding and she could react clearly and with confidence.

Colo could have ended up being labeled a "problem horse" like so many others; in the wrong hands she would have been a horse who needed to be taught a lesson. Strong tactics would have been used and this would have been exactly the wrong thing to do, it would have brought out more anxiety and anger.

Thankfully Colo has a home for life with a wonderful mum who wants to understand her and help her.

It makes you think doesn't it? I can think of a lot of horses who have hard treatment because they don't "listen", more and more gadgets are used. When all that was needed was understanding and patience after all it is mankind who have tampered with the breeding to get the best horse, to boost their ego, trouble is when it goes wrong mans ego is hurt and when this happens life can become unbearable for the horse.

WILLOW

Willow is ten years old and has been with her owner Sue for 6 years, as Sue was completing the paperwork I connected with willow and introduced myself. I picked up the energy of Willow straight away, she is a dominant strong willed mare, all of this I knew before I had even laid my hands on her. I followed Sue into the stable and watched her put the head collar on, Willow put her ears back and shook her head. I stood back talking to Sue so that willow had a chance to get used to my energy. I held my hands out to Willow telling her I would not hurt her and asking permission to step forward. Willow was a little agitated, she knows her own mind and does not put up with fools. I asked Willow if I could touch her and she agreed, I slowly scanned her over. I realised that Willow used her face pulling to control her personal space, if anyone comes near she looks like she will savage you, but, it is an act that she puts on to keep people away.

As I scanned her over I felt heat in her left shoulder and both sides behind the pelvis, also on the right in her ribs. Once willow relaxed and accepted my energy she started to communicate by showing me pictures, they were quite disturbing. Willow was, running in blind panic, bolting, she was running through fencing and anything that got in her way. She showed me a picture of a dog barking and chasing her, Willow was very scared and I could feel her fear within me. I turned to Sue and told her what I had been shown, she said "oh my god she just told you that?" Sue was amazed, and continued to tell me about an incident when Willow had bolted, they were out riding when a dog leapt out and tried to bite Willow the dog then chased her. Sue had fallen off and was quite badly injured and Willow had bolted home going through fencing and jumping anything else that got in her way.

I told Sue that Willow is very strong willed and a herd leader. If she was in the wild she would be the lead mare, she is very sensitive to energy, she is always on alert and her behavior can change due to the people around her or even if the weather is about to change. I carried on healing Willow who had now become very relaxed, allowing me in. I put my hand in front of Willow's mouth and she started sucking my fingers like a foal would. The feeling I had from Willow was huge sadness and loss I then felt that there had been a sudden weaning and Willow was holding emotion from this. I told Sue this and she said that Willow had stayed with her Mum until she was four and then her Mum had had an accident and was put to sleep. I felt that Willow did not understand what had happened to her Mum and Sue was not sure if Willow had seen the body of the mare. Although the weaning was later in life it has still affected Willow, one minute Mum was there then she was gone. As we were talking about this Willow started licking and chewing and yawning as the tension left her body.

Willow has a strong connection with Sue, she knows her inside out. Willow told me that she has not been seeing so much of Sue and she misses her. She enjoyed their long rides together when they are as one, but the rides have been short lately. Willow also said that "Sue needs to listen to her own inner voice and trust herself more and not listen to other people". Willow told me that they been through similar situations in life and they have grown strong together. Sue by now had a tear in her eye and could not believe all that Willow was saying. She has been working more lately and so time with Willow had been limited, she had been told by her instructor she could cut down the length of rides that they were going on as Willow was very fit. She also confirmed that they had been through a lot together. Willow also told me that Sue should teach, I asked Sue about this and she said that the dream was to teach young children in school, it seemed Willow was pushing her towards her dream goal.

As I carried on healing a man walked towards Willow's box and her ears went back and the energy from the mare changed straight away. She was very angry, I asked Sue to see if she could ask the man to leave as there was no way I could carry on healing with him near Willow. As he walked away I burst out laughing Sue wanted to know what Willow had said I told her she had called him an "***hole," Sue burst out laughing and explained that the man in question had backed Willow and pushed her to hard until there had been a big disagreement and he had been thrown off by Willow.

I changed sides and worked on the area by her ribs, I felt as if the wind had been knocked out of me and I was sure she must have fallen. Sue confirmed that Willow had seriously hurt herself when the dog had chased her, she had fallen and been severely winded. I carried on healing and Willow let go of the anxiety and yawned and yawned as her story was told. After the healing I walked out to the field where I could see Willow really shine as she lifted her tail and galloped around the field full of spirit and life - beautiful

Sometimes Horses know you better than you know yourself, a lot of appointments can become quite personal, about the rider/owner. The horse will give me information to make their owner open up and talk about their problems. Sometimes it is a healing not only for the horse but for the owner as well. Emotions can be released and a joint healing takes place.

SAM

I introduced myself to Sam and scanned him over I felt straight away that Sam was a very strong character; he had the most beautiful energy running down through his body. Sam knows who and what he is and is very confident in himself, he has been in the same home for ten years and because of this he is very secure within himself. Never under estimate how constant change of homes affects a horse, the horses that stay in a home for many years become much more grounded and secure.

When Lyn, Sam's owner was taking off his rug he started talking straight away, he told me that he is happy being ridden in straight lines and not so keen on circles. I asked Sam if I could heal him and he was happy for me to scan him over. His body felt great until I got to his pelvis where I felt heat from an old injury which was causing tension and stiffness. I showed Lyn what I was feeling by dowsing over Sam, the pendulum was still and quiet until we got to the pelvis there it started to move confirming what I was feeling. I also felt that his energy is older than his years and felt that perhaps he had done too much when first backed putting pressure on his joints.

Lyn then went to get another coat and I stood with Sam and actually talked about the weather!! He told me he would rather be out in the field rugged up than stabled, he hates being in and is quite content out and sheltering by the hedge. I told Lyn about this when she returned and she laughed and confirmed that he is much happier out. I carried on healing him and felt a block in his shoulder which I worked on, he showed me a picture of him with a young rider and they were competing x country. He looked very fit, buzzing with energy, he loved the partnership with his rider and the fun of competing. He told me that he had a huge connection with the rider and loved his work. "Then it all changed" he said "with the new rider there is no connection". I spoke to Lyn about this who confirmed that her eldest daughter had competed Sam and they had a lovely connection but she has now moved away and recently her younger sister has been trying to ride him. She is keen to compete him but there time together has not been easy!

 This explained the liking straight lines and not circles, I told Lyn that her daughter had to develop feel with him, to think what she wanted to happen before asking. He needed to be introduced to the work slowly and your daughter has to accept that he will not find the big jumps easy anymore, they need to find a level of work they are both happy with. Sam enjoyed the relationship he had with the eldest daughter they looked after each other, if she missed something he would see it and if his rider got the stride wrong he would correct it, they had been a team and a team that worked well.

His new rider needs to become more connected with Sam and learn to listen, i.e. think what you want to happen then less leg will be needed. The two girls' are different personalities his new rider needs to be more open and listen to Sam. If he decides that he cannot do something it is for a reason and his age needs to be taken into consideration, if he is aching he will not be happy to work so feel and understanding needs to be developed. Sam can look after himself, he can be quite stubborn if he feels things are not right then Lyn needs to ask why he will not do something rather than thinking he is being naughty.

Lyn told me that her daughter had fallen off Sam and her confidence has been knocked, but the fall happened because Sam had pain in his back not because he was being naughty. I was now healing his pelvis and he did not show me the fall but showed a picture of hounds in his field, he panicked and galloped, when turning, his hind quarters slipped away and twisted his pelvis which caused pain down through his back. Sam has been treated by a physio and is now on the road to recovery

I love treating horses who have been in the same home for most of their life they communicate really clearly. One question Lyn had was is he happy and I could reply with a big Yes.

NIGEL

Nigel is a Clydesdale which is a heavy horse and would have been used years ago for pulling carts and ploughs. I arrived knowing that Nigel suffers with separation anxiety; Helen his owner had contacted me to see if healing could help him. Helen was also desperate to form a better partnership with Nigel as he kept her at arm's length.

Nigel is a big horse 17hands in height, I introduced myself to him and started scanning his body, apart from his shoulders where I felt heat, it was as if the rest of his body was switched off. He had huge barriers around him that he had put up to protect himself. Nigel also suffers with "shivers" so is not very strong on his hind legs, every time my hands went anywhere near his pelvis tremors would go down his hind quarters. I dowsed over Nigel so that Helen could see the difference in Nigel's energy down each side. On the left the pendulum was very quiet but on the right as I moved it down his body it spiraled very quickly.

As we were talking about what I had found and felt, Nigel showed me his party trick, he tries to push you away with his head! I felt there was a relationship problem between Helen and Nigel and asked her about this. "He just doesn't seem to like me or want me anywhere near him" she replied. I took the rope and started healing Nigel. The barriers were huge, he had locked himself away in a safe place. I asked him if I could help him and he showed me pictures of being in a barn. He was on his own, very unhappy and miserable his head hung low and his body and mind were switched off. I felt that he was left unhandled for a long time and then when the time came for attention it was very forceful. He showed me a time when people came and caught him and he did not want them near him he was very scared. A twitch had been brought out and his lip had been clamped in the rope, as it turned and the rope became tighter his lip felt like it was on fire. Everything had been hard, there had been no gentleness or compassion; he then showed me lots of people riding him. I can only explain what I was seeing as a trekking centre where Nigel had been overworked. Because in Nigel's words he had been the dependable plod, he was safe and the weight carrier so anyone who could not ride was put on Nigel.

As Nigel was sharing his life story he was walking around and trying to swipe me with his head, I walked around with him and carried on healing trying to sooth him and get through the barriers. Round and round the yard we went all of his anger showing in every stride. As we continued to walk he showed me pictures of himself with Helen. The pictures showed Nigel panicking, going through fencing knocking Helen over as he went. I related this to Helen, she let out a sigh and confirmed that Nigel had panicked when his friend had been taken for a ride, he had smashed through the fencing to reach him. Unfortunately Helen was in the way and she had been injured. As a result of this Helen has become nervous of Nigel and she has her own barriers up resulting in them bouncing of each other.

Helen was desperate to form a bond and lasting relationship with Nigel, but since the accident there is now one fearful and anxious, the other stressed and angry because of the feelings of the other one. Nigel is picking up on this so they are in a never ending circle. I spent a long time talking to Nigel and telling him that he was now safe and in a forever home and that he needed to learn to relax. Every so often his eyes would become heavy as he felt the healing energy, but within a minute he pulled himself out of the relaxed state and the barrier came down again.

I knew something had to be done to try and convince Nigel, I could see how worried Helen was about him and I asked her to place her hand on his shoulder. I then placed my hand on her shoulder and then on Nigel. I told Helen to tell Nigel in her mind how much she loved him and that he was safe. I then asked her to imagine love flowing out of her hand and into Nigel. We stayed like this for a while and gradually bit by bit Nigel's energy came down and then at long last with a big sigh the barriers disappeared and he relaxed. His head hung low and his eyes closed as he let go of all the anguish held deep inside. He licked and chewed and went into a beautiful healing doze looking like he had been sedated by a vet.

Nigel stayed like this for a long while so I carried on healing and when he started to come out of the healing he yawned the biggest yawns as his body energy rebalanced and the blocks disappeared. Nigel had had a huge healing and so had Helen they now needed to keep the barriers down and build a trusting and loving relationship.

I visited Nigel six months later and I am pleased to report that he is happy and relaxed and now has a wonderful relationship with Helen.

6

WHERE HAVE WE GONE WRONG?

Where have we gone wrong? This is a question I ask myself all the time, when did we stop listening or have we ever really listened. I believe that people listened and had a greater connection with their horses when they worked as a team, when they were used on the farms, docks and mines. Failing to listen then would have brought a breakdown in the team and the work would have suffered. They both had to have respect for each other, to listen and feel. Where as we as a society over the years have switched off our senses; we live in an electric world where nothing needs to be felt any more. We spend our time in our head and have long forgotten about living from the heart. As a society we have become so guarded from being hurt that we have huge barriers around us that stop us feeling. We live and are guided by an ego, in a world where material objects have taken over from our natural senses. We are born with six senses but most of these have now been blocked, if we cannot see, hear and touch all that is around us what chance does that little inner voice and intuition have?

We live in a fast world; we never have enough time, we run around like headless chickens always chasing the next dream, the next deal. For some they never even get started and feel inadequate and left behind in a society that no longer breaths. I sometimes feel they are the lucky ones, ok they are not chasing the ego, they have no need for the big cars and houses and endless holidays. For them life is lived in the moment, they cannot afford the dreams of wealth and luxury. The moment for them is making every penny count. They have no barriers their senses are alive and well and they listen to their intuition. They feel the hug from their children and the love of their partner, they hear the birdsong and they feel the energy of their horse. Life can be hard and the tears fall, all of these emotions they feel and it makes them whole. Just beneath the surface of all of this is that little inner voice the one that talks sense, the one that does not have time for pipe dreams but the one that is always right and if followed will help you at every turn on your journey through life.

People value their lives by what they have, not their inner beauty and feelings, but material wealth. To get the material wealth and tick off the wish list they multi task from the time the alarm clock goes off, every second is worked in some way. Their eyes are locked on to modern technology and their ears plugged with the sound of noise. They go through the day at 100 miles an hour because every second every minute is valued not in a beautiful way but as money. So while their eyes and ears are locked onto the next deal they fail to hear the wonders and sights of Mother Nature all around them.

Society is so busy doing, that we never have time to just be, this is why people are failing to hear their horses. They have become disconnected with life and all that goes on around them. The people who live in the moment who are happy with their life and are not forever chasing rainbows, these are the people who can truly connect. When they go to their horses they have done their days work, which enables them to live, then they switch off and enjoy their horse. Their mind is focused on just one thing their horse, to feel their soft hair and the warmth of their skin. To hear the neigh as the horse turns and sees them and to see their beautiful horse come to them to greet them. It fills their body with warmth and love and relaxation, their time is spent enjoying every second and connecting, really connecting with their horse. Whether they are just brushing them or riding on a loose rein out in the countryside the connection is there. They breathe in time with their horse as they become one. Both listening and feeling each other and everything that surrounds them.

We need a better balance; I have lost count of the times I have watched people arrive at yards to find their horse has been brought in for them. They walk straight to the tack room and come out with the required gadgets and tack their horses up. Often there is no word of communication unless the horse turns away or becomes awkward, and then the person finds their voice. They demand that their horse stands for them and doesn't move; they after all pay all the bills and keep the horse in the luxury of his stable 23 hours a day. Their horse should be grateful and want to be schooled and do as it is told so that as a pair they look amazing and people look twice. But does the owner feel any gratitude towards their horse? I think not, they are using the horse as an ego tool like a new car, it looks good. So they wonder why their horse switches off and becomes as disconnected as them, the horse mirrors the attitude of their owner. They have come from the office stressed and have one whole hour to spare and they expect their horse to perform. The stress from the day is held within their bodies and this is the communication that the horse reads. A horse would naturally move away from anything that is angry, the horse feels the stress, the anger bubbling under the surface and his senses all six of them that he lives by are on high alert. Their intuition tells them this person is not a good person to be with. They are not a leader or a partner and the horse would want to escape and get away.

So the tension builds, the horse does not work properly because the tension causes blocks within his body, the rider becomes even more tense and angry until it is all the fault of the horse. The spurs are dug in the whip is used, all because that rider has no feeling left. The barriers they have put up to stop them feeling anything deep within stops them being able to feel "horse".

Years ago I had a livery yard and I was often disturbed about things that I saw and one day it went too far. I had a livery that was very stressed in her life; she would come up to the yard and have an hour to school her horse. She shouted at it as she tacked it up because it moved away from her and as the lady became angrier the horse in turn became more stressed. She took her horse into the school, mounted, by now the mare was as stressed as the lady was angry. Because of the stress the horse was finding it difficult to move through her body, the ladies energy was solid and her face rigid. The more she asked of the mare the more it couldn't do, until she started to use her whip. It was too much for the mare and she promptly bucked and bucked until the lady was on the floor.

I was called as someone had witnessed the accident and as I came round the corner I will never forget what I saw, the lady had picked herself up and grabbed the reins of the now frightened horse. She then proceeded to shout at the horse "how dare you buck me off" and then started whipping the mare. It took two of us to stop her, I grabbed the horse and someone else took hold of the lady and removed the whip. I told the lady to leave my yard and I took the shaking horse into the stables where I bathed the marks left by the whip and spoke quietly to her until she calmed down. That evening the lady contacted me and apologised, she explained that her life was a mess and she had very little spare time and she expected her horse to work for her in the spare time that she had. I told her that her life needed sorting out as there was no way her horse could work with her in the state that she is in. I looked after the horse for a month which gave the lady time to sort out the problems in her life and realise what she had done.

I am sure that there will be a lot of you who are reading this book who can think of an incident that you have witnessed and felt uncomfortable about. A better balance needs to be found, we need to take a breath and reconnect with ourselves before we try and connect with horses. The best place to rebalance and connect is out with Mother Nature and in the presence of your horse. Take a look around you, breathe, not the short shallow breaths that we have become used to, but actually fill your lungs. Notice the colors and sounds and see the world as your horse does. Quiet the mind and be in the moment, let your mind clear and just be. Meditation is a useful tool to bring you back into your body and reawaken your senses. It is a time you just give to yourself, it doesn't come easy and takes practice but when you reach deep within and feel at peace you realise how tired and switched off you have become. The fog of everyday life will start to lift as you find yourself, you will become more relaxed and in a place that your horse can accept you and be happy in your company. Suddenly the horse is pleased to see you, easier to catch, your rides are pure pleasure because you are working in harmony.

You can not fool your horse! You can turn up at the yard with a happy face and looking like you have no worries but deep inside the stress of the day is still there. It is that stress inside that the horses read, not the surface smile, but the inner energy that cannot change until we do.

The best example I can give of this is my own experience, my father was very ill and in hospital, he didn't have long to live. I was juggling driving to the hospital looking after my family and animals and pretending I was coping. I would turn up at the yard and tell everyone I was ok. But to my horses I wasn't, my two girls' Grace and Sammy were box walking and very stressed in my company. I led them up to the field and let them go but they didn't run away Sammy kicked up her hind legs and double barreled me in the hip bringing me down in the mud. I sat there in the muddy gateway and cried not only from the pain but also from the grief held in my heart about my Dad. My horses stood over me licking and chewing and yawning releasing my pain to the universe. When I was spent and my tears had stopped the girls' sighed and walked away, I was back with them, the barrier had been taken down and the emotion released. I crawled out of the field and promised myself that I would not shelve my tears I would release them as tears are a healing. Emotion kept in becomes a black tar clogging your energy system until it becomes full.

Horses are amazing healers if you release your emotions they will help you heal and become calm.

7

JUST BECAUSE

Sometimes I am called to treat a horse as their owner wants them to have a healing and to know that their horse is happy. Not all horses have problems some have had a wonderful life and this shows in the healing………………………………..

TJ

TJ is a lovely shire; he is 19 years old and is loved to bits by his two mums Laura and Becky.   Becky introduced me to TJ who she called her war horse, I stopped her there. TJ had already started communicating and had told me that he had been a war horse! Becky was amazed that she had picked up on this information and I was pleased to tell her that she is one of life's communicators.

I scanned TJ over and knew that he had a lot to say, he had heat in his joints which he told me was as a result of the years. I asked him if I could heal his body and he licked and chewed and rested his hind leg, so I started on his left side. For a while TJ stood and enjoyed the healing and a huge feeling of peace came from him.

TJ is an old soul meaning he has lived before, from what he told me he has been on this earth two times before. The first time he was a working horse on a farm, it was a family farm and he showed me the farmer and also his children. The farmer was wearing clothing made of a heavy wool and he wore big laced up boots and an old jacket with parches on the elbows. TJ worked on the farm and felt huge respect and love for the farmer and the work that they did together. They worked as a team and TJ was very much part of the family, highly valued, for without him they could not farm. The hours were long the work often hard but they worked together and he was well treated, fed and loved. He knew that the family valued him and appreciated all that he did and as a result of this he worked as hard as he could. This was a good life a happy time.

The second time he was indeed a war horse but not on the frontline, he showed me the docks and from the sound of the voices it was London, he was used to take the cargo to the big ships. He showed me the ships they were huge steam ships with big funnels, there was lots of banter and laughter between the people working the docks.   He was well looked after and he showed me the feed bag that he was fed from. Again the work was long and hard but they all worked hard, his owner worked alongside him every minute they toiled, there was huge respect for each other. As TJ was showing me the pictures of his life he was relaxed and licking and chewing and yawning the biggest of yawns. I have to tell you that while TJ was talking to me it was like a Grandfather speaking of long ago memories when times were hard but at the same time good, there was respect and plenty of team work and people pulling together.

I then changed sides and started working on the right side of his neck, I could feel tremendous heat under my hand and I asked Becky to run her hand down so that she could feel it. I started working through the heat and TJ changed completely. He became very angry his eyes became hard and he started snatching at grass in a very anxious way. Becky was quite shocked in the change in him I reassured her that it would be ok and carried on healing. I soon realised that we had hit this life, TJ has had a real shock in this life he cannot believe how things have changed. He bit his side and I put my hand on the place, as I did TJ showed me pictures of his side, it had been very sore. I felt that the sores had been caused by a driving harness and asked Becky, who confirmed that this would have been where the driving shafts would go.

TJ carried on "They worked me hard, this was no surprise I am a working horse but there was no thanks no working as a team just more hard work, you are not respected for what you contribute and the work means nothing". All the time this was going on TJ was showing anger in every way he could. He stamped the ground, took huge bites of the air, I apologised to TJ for how the world now treated horses and assured him that I was trying to make people realise that things need to change. He slowly calmed down and I gave him a lovely healing soothing over the anger of this life.

TJ now has a lovely home where he is loved and valued, his owner first saw him giving wagon rides to tourists and knew that she had to buy him to make his life better. This she has done, but for TJ the disappointment of this life is a lesson for us all. Horses are not here for our amusement to be picked up and put down when we have had enough, they think and feel the same as humans, there are people who will argue this fact with me until they are blue in the face, but, when a horse tells you how sad life has become in this world perhaps we should all start to listen..........................

I was lucky enough to heal TJ again about six months later something I am very grateful for because in the Autumn of 2012 he died of colic.

LOLA

Lola, is a 27year old Thoroughbred who in spirit does not feel her age but her body is feeling the years. Her owner Suzie was quite worried about my visit and had been wondering what her horse would tell me!

I introduced myself to Lola and she was very impatient for me to start "get on with it, get on with it" came through loud and clear. I scanned Lola's body moving my hand over her, Lola was happier when I was on her right side, when I was on her left she became slightly agitated. I moved slowly letting her get used to my energy and telling her that I would not hurt her. As you would expect of a horse the age of Lola there was heat in her joints, the right side of her pelvis had energy blocks and her knees were badly damaged. Whilst I was doing this Lola started talking and was very matter of fact she told me she is old but she is fine. She is a very grand lady, practically royalty and I was very grateful for being allowed to treat her.

I changed sides to the left, I felt tremendous heat in Lola's neck and down into her shoulder; Lola told me that she knew the shoulder was not right. Lola is in a lovely place she has a beautiful energy some would describe as an aura around her. I decided to dowse on Lola as I felt that she was only showing me what she wanted me to see and that there was more going on. Suzie could see that the left side of Lola was very blocked, the pendulum was spiraling and on the right it hardly moved apart from over the pelvis where there is an old injury. I was able to tell Suzie that Lola's energy is younger than her years. The picture she showed me was of herself in full bloom, bouncing and full of energy. Lola then relaxed and showed me pictures of a grass and jumps and I asked Suzie if she had evented and she said yes before she came to her Lola had been very successful.

Lola became quiet and I healed her legs, whilst I was doing this my spirit guide told me how her tendons had been damaged in the past but they had healed well. At this point Lola needed to have a drink which a lot of horses do during a healing it flushes everything through. Lola licked and chewed and yawned, Lola is very much a lady! and Suzie has done very well keeping Lola so happy and healthy. When Lola settled again I carried on and Lola told me that she had taught Suzie everything. She made me feel that Suzie had been a very inexperienced rider and Lola had guided and taught her. I told Suzie this and she laughed and told Lola not to be so cheeky, it appears that Suzie trained with the Spanish Riding School and is very highly trained!.

I then concentrated on the left where Lola needed lots of healing, there was a scar on Lola's leg and I asked her about this. "My leg was caught in wire" her voice told me how disgusted she was that it had been anywhere near her! She showed me the wire and continued "no one came I was there for ages" Suzie explained that it happened at night and Lola was noticed first thing in the morning. Lola carried on communicating in pictures, she has a lovely presence and adored people looking at her. The picture was of Lola doing dressage "I loved it but sometimes perhaps I may have been a little bit too enthusiastic!!" I told Suzie this and she laughed confirming that Lola could put on quite a show. Lola then showed me that her left side had taken the force of every fall, one fall she had collided with a solid fence and her shoulder took the full force, this is why it is damaged. Lola then became quiet and very sleepy as she took the healing energy in, I worked on the knee and shoulder and moving the energy blocks through her body, Lola yawned and licked and chewed as the healing was absorbed. Lola showed me the leg bandaged and that she had been on box rest after a fall but the healing wasn't complete and she had been worked too soon resulting in more damage in the leg.

Lola became quite angry at this point, she showed me how she was hurt whilst jumping, it was almost like her body crumpled, the front stopped but the back didn't. It was this that took her from the beautiful bouncy flowing horse she was to one who ached and didn't flow as before. She made known to me her feelings about the situation and I gave her a moment to calm down, when she had relaxed Lola accepted the healing.   Lola was a much more serious horse on her left side telling us about her injuries and showing her emotions as a result.

I carried on healing Lola and she became very sleepy, releasing her emotions, her body energy clearing had drained her and I kept stopping as I did not want Lola to fall down, Lola licked and chewed and yawned.

I went back to treat Lola again as her body had been through a tough life and I wanted to give her another healing to help her with her aches and pains. Suzie makes sure Lola has everything she needs from magnotherapy blankets to a whole wardrobe of rugs!. Lola isn't ridden anymore and Suzie has made sure her last years have made up for the life that she had before.

COOPER

I was booked to go and see a Shetland pony, his owner Karen filled out the form, which I didn't read as I was occupied talking to Cooper over his stable door. I entered his stable thinking he was a miniature Shetland, anyone who knows me is aware that I have two mini's of my own and they never cease to amaze me just how perfect "horse" they are. I let Cooper sniff my hand and waited for him to accept my energy, it was then that I noticed something different. I went back and read the form and read what Karen had written about him. One of the questions on the form is about health and she had put that he has "dwarfism". Cooper has the length of body of a standard Shetland but smaller round the middle and shorter legs. He completely melted my heart. I said to Karen that I have never come across dwarfism before and she told me that normally they would have been put down at birth. All I can say is thank god they gave Cooper the chance of life

I got down to Cooper's level on my knees and asked him if I could heal him. I started healing Cooper and felt down his legs. He has enlarged knees due to the dwarfism and from what I was shown by my guides it is almost like his knees are becoming to big for the socket and Karen needs to watch for dislocation. Due to this he has aches in his legs and his knees can be stiff. I spent quite a while healing his knees and he licked and chewed and yawned. I let him have a little break and then asked him where he would like me to heal next. He pulled my attention to his right shoulder by biting it indicating to me that he wanted healing which I did. I healed my way down his right side; every time I tried to heal his left side he would walk away and turn to block me. He was showing me aggression and I didn't want to overpower him with my energy so I told him that was fine and sat back in the straw; I told him that when he was ready I would carry on.

After a short time he looked at me, I kept my body energy low and very slowly he reversed back into me and I placed my hands on his pelvis. He then allowed me to heal his left side; he had heat down through his spine which showed me that the area needed healing as his energy was blocked. I asked Karen to place her hand on the area so she could feel the heat, I worked on releasing it and as I did Cooper reacted with lots of yawning and licking and chewing.

I placed my hands on Cooper's head and he told me that his skull was tight, he has an enlarged head due to his condition and it sometimes aches. Cooper is very sensitive to energy, all of his senses are highly tuned, you could not shout and be angry with him because he would not cope. Everything has to be black and white no grey areas, you need to give him time to absorb, think, and then act you cannot expect instant reactions. He finds the high energy of children hard to cope with and they should SBT- stop, breath, think – before they go to him. This will bring their energy down before approaching Cooper and they will get a better response from him. Everything has to be in, Cooper time, slowly and then he is ok. He is the most adorable chap and a delight to treat and very lucky to be with a family who understand him.

BILL

I visited a lovely Cob called Bill, Kate his owner had booked me to visit him because she wanted to make sure Bill was happy and to hopefully find out a little bit more about him. I introduced myself to Bill who is a very laid back chap, he allowed me to scan over his body. He had energy blocks in the right shoulder making the shoulder stiff I explained to Kate that what I was feeling would make it difficult for Bill to turn corners making schooling difficult. Bill told me that he doesn't really think much of the schooling and would much rather go on a buckle plod around the block. He told me that he needs Kate to trust him and have more confidence in their partnership. Bill told me that he and Kate were meant to be together she needed him and he her. I told Kate about this and she confirmed that she had first seen Bill at a dealers and had taken to long making a decision and he had been sold to somebody else. Kate then brought another cob who tragically had died after they had only been together for six months. After a while Kate decided that she wanted another horse in her life and returned to the dealers to see what they had. She went through the gate turned the corner and there was Bill, it seems that he was not forward going enough for his owners and they had returned him. Kate wasted no time and secured the deal having Bill delivered that week.

Bill is a real gentleman, he briefly showed me a past life where he had a working life and everything was very routine, you knew your job and got on with it. If you worked hard you would be fed and watered with a nice bed at the end of the day. Like a lot of old Souls, they have found life this time around a lot different.

I carried on healing and Bill came back to this life, he showed me pictures of a horse lorry with writing on the side and the word Ireland in big letters. He told me that this is where he had come from, the pictures continued as his life story was told. He showed me that he had been herded into the lorry with other horses looking at him; he would have only been about 18 months old. He was very leggy, quiet and lacking in confidence, he showed me how he always stood at the back waiting for the others to finish eating and he would have what was left. He is very intelligent in this way, he soon learnt how to stay out of trouble with other horses and men, he would never argue and would accept all that was given to him both good and bad. Bill then showed me that he was used as a tourist ride pulling carts full of people on holiday; he had been worked hard and suffered with sore feet. He showed me that his feet were cut back and iodine poured over them. His feet were so sore he fell, he showed me his right shoulder jarring. I gave him a lot of healing on his right side and after a long while he accepted it and licked and chewed. It was almost as if he didn't feel that he deserved to take the healing, if there was someone else to have given it to he would have passed it straight on.

I carried on healing and felt heat around the wither area and Bill showed me that there have been issues with a saddle causing pain. I mentioned this to Kate who confirmed that when the saddle had been checked it had been tight, the saddler had reflocked it so that he would be more comfortable.

Kate asked me if she could ask Bill a question, I said we could try but there are no guarantees of an answer. Kate wanted to know why he bucks when asked to canter. Bill replied that he has never really been taught to canter and with his build he finds it difficult, if you hold him up together with the reins this puts pressure on the base of his neck and down his right shoulder, he likes the reins to be long. Kate also wanted to know why he didn't seem to enjoy the rides on the common. Straight away Bill showed me pictures of big green open spaces and how he felt very insecure. He had only ever known riding round roads or tracks and he didn't feel safe in open fields.

Kate's daughters phone then started ringing and he became quite cross, "she never listens, she needs to be with us 100% and be quiet then she will learn" wise words from the horses mouth. Bill then relaxed into the healing and went off into a beautiful healing doze. When I had finished he licked and chewed and yawned as he released and his energy started flowing.

Bill needs to value himself a little more, in the forever home that he now has I think he will start to do this. I look forward to seeing the pictures of him being shown in hand, he does have the most impressive feathers and beautiful long mane.

PETE

Jane had booked me to come and see her horse Pete, she felt that he was not truly happy and wanted to know what she could do to make his life better.

I arrived to find Pete with his pony companion sunning themselves on the yard, we took Pete into the stable so that we wouldn't be bothered by the flies and I asked him if I could heal him. He wasn't to sure at first and moved away from me, Jane told him off but I told her it was ok I can be a bit of a shock to some horses and the healing couldn't happen unless a horse is happy and open to it.

I spent time talking to Pete and very slowly he started to relax, I asked Pete if I could touch him and moved my hand towards his shoulder. He didn't move away so I touched his shoulder and when he was comfortable with my energy I started scanning his body with my eye and hand. When I felt over his withers they twitched violently and I could not put my hand on the area. I then felt pain in my shoulder which wasn't mine but coming from Pete. I could feel in my body that he was very sore down his shoulder, he then showed me pictures of a lady riding him, the saddle was very tight so tight that he showed me that the nerves in the wither area had been damaged. I told Jane about this and told her that I didn't think it was her riding as the lady looked larger. Jane laughed and said it was her "I have lost weight" she said "the saddle had been tight and I hadn't realised". The saddle had been changed and the physio now regularly treats Pete. I carried on healing the wither area releasing the memory of the pain until he felt more comfortable.

I carried on healing down through his body and Pete seemed very relaxed and happy to accept the healing. When I got to the right hind he suddenly changed he became agitated and tense, I could feel huge amounts of heat in the flank area and he tried to kick me. I explained to Jane that he was holding anger within his body about the pain and this is what he was showing me. The anger needs to be shown and released before he can let the memory go and be healed. Jane was shocked as she had never seen him behave like this before, I assured her it was ok and I carried on healing. His leg was scarred so I knew there had been an injury and I asked Pete about it, "I don't know why he did it" he said, and he showed me a picture of another horse, he was out in the field with him they were grazing when all of a sudden the other horse turned on Pete and kicked out catching his leg. The pain in his leg as the metal shoe caught his skin was immense, the cut had gone deep. The force of the kick had caused internal damage and Jane told me that Pete had been rushed to the equine hospital where he stayed for a week. The accident had changed his life, his friend who had kicked him had been moved from the yard so when Pete returned he was no longer there. This had caused a huge hole in Pete's life, apart from that one incident the two horses had always got on well and had been kept together for a number of years.

As a result of the kick Pete's life had changed, his friend had disappeared and also Pete's routine. As a result of the damage to the leg Pete had a number of weeks on box rest, when the leg had healed he was allowed out again. But there was to be no more hunting or jumping just gentle hacking. Pete showed me pictures of him and Jane competing and they were a good team. "But it all stopped" he was very angry about this and the energy block caused by the anger was making his leg stiff. I worked on the leg, dodging the kicks until his anger was spent. When he became quiet and the healing reached him his energy dropped and he began licking and chewing and yawning, the energy shifted within and the anger was replaced with peace. I carried on healing and placed my hands on his head, here I felt sadness not only for the loss of his friend and the life that he had known but also because the relationship between Jane and Pete has changed and he misses her.

As Pete was relaxing I told Jane what Pete had said and she confirmed that he had been kicked by his stable friend and it had caused nerve damage restricting them to a hacking life. At the same time Jane found out she was pregnant so she could see why he had told me his life had changed. Instead of spending her time with Pete she now had children and life had changed completely. Instead of coming to the stables and visiting Pete on her own, more often than not she had one or two of her young children with her. Jane was shocked at how the change had affected Pete and how much anger he had been holding in his body, she also began to understand how their relationship had totally changed. Pete had been Jane's number one but when she married and had children her priorities had to change and she did not realise quite what an impact this has had on Pete

I turned to Pete and placed my hand on his shoulder and told him that the children were here to stay and that Jane was now aware of how he felt and that she would allow one to one time again. Pete is jealous of the children and after the healing Jane told me that in the past Pete had tried to kick her son, making her feel angry. They had got into a vicious circle and this wasn't being helped by Pete having what I can only describe as a mid-life crisis.

Jane contacted me the following week and said that she is spending more time with Pete, she has arranged for a child minder and is now hacking him a couple of times a week. She admitted that she is enjoying Pete's company and hadn't realised just how much she had missed being with him. Jane commented that Pete's eye was softer and she could now touch his wither without it twitching.

KAI

I received a phone call from Jill a client of mine in Devon asking me to revisit her Arab Kai, he had not been well since my last visit and she was worried about him.

Kai is now retired, he had been a very successful endurance horse, he is in his mid twenties and due to his working life he has arthritic joints but he told me on an earlier visit that he had loved the riding. I greeted Kai and he sniffed my hands and he seemed pleased to see me, he looked very well and had put on weight since our last healing.

I started healing Kai and he started yawning straight away he loves being healed and finds the whole experience very relaxing. As I started healing down his right hand side the word colic came into my head. I carried on healing him, when I got to his pelvis I was given kidneys, urine infection, I asked Jill if she had noticed that he had been having problems passing water or passing more than normal. "She laughed and said "how did you know" I told her that that was what I had been told! She confirmed that he had recently had a blockage and also had colic.

I carried on healing Kai, he started walking around his stable and was showing signs of anxiety. Not about the healing but about having to pass urine. I placed my hand near his sheath and could feel that it had been very painful to wee, because of this he stopped himself going. His mind was still telling him that it would hurt. I told him to relax and breathe and it would be ok, Jill and I went out of his stable to give him some privacy. Kai kept walking round his stable and stopping then he would move on again and this went on for about ten minutes. I returned to the door and told him to relax he looked at me, stood still, spread his legs, took a big breath and then sure enough he passed water.

During the healing I found heat in his neck and as I was healing the area I felt an intense pain over my left eye, I put my hand by his head and he placed his head in my hands so that I could give him healing around the eye. I told Jill about this and she has since spoken to her vet who has confirmed that damage in the neck can cause pain in the head and eye so they are watching this.
Kai is a lovely old horse and I am pleased to say made a full recovery from the urine infection and the colic. Unfortunately healing cannot turn back time and in the Autumn of 2013 Kai passed to spirit, he had a very happy life and I am sure will come back again.

LOONA

I was booked to go to Wiltshire to treat a welsh mare called Loona, her owner Sarah didn't have any major concerns about Loona but wanted to know how she was feeling. Before I treated Loona I treated Sarah's mum's gelding, throughout the healing Loona kept making her presence known by let's say, passing wind. It soon came to her turn and Sarah went in and put a lovely pink sparkling head collar on Loona, as I walked into the stable I heard loud and clear "I hate pink!" I burst out laughing and told Sarah who laughed and said "but she has everything in pink".

I introduced myself to Loona who carried on talking, telling me that him over there, meaning the gelding I had just treated, gets lots more than me. I told Sarah this and she explained that Loona has to have limited food because of her figure as she is too fat, Loona replied "Look who's talking, have you seen her!!" I laughed and decided that Sarah had a good sense of humour and passed on the message, Sarah was in tears through laughing. Loona then told me to ask about the pink jodhpurs and showed me a picture of Sarah wearing them, I took a deep breath and asked Sarah what colour jodhpurs she rode in "black" came her reply. I breathed a sigh of relief and said, not pink, Sarah and her mum laughed and confirmed that the favorite colour last year had been "PINK". I told her that Loona was glad it was now black as the pink ones did nothing for her figure!!

When I had stopped laughing I asked Loona if I could heal her and placed my hand on her shoulder. I immediately felt heat and asked Sarah if she would check her saddle and make sure it wasn't too tight. Loona also showed me pictures of Sarah sitting to the left, so I asked her to get someone to look from behind when she is riding to make sure she is sitting even, as this was making Loona unbalanced. I carried on healing the area until the heat had gone. Loona then showed me a picture of a tall very thin lady who had owned her before Sarah. The pictures showed Loona being shown by the lady and I had a feeling of contentment come over me, Loona had been happy when she had been with the lady. I was then showed pictures of foals out in the field, from this I felt that the lady I had been shown had bred Loona, it had been the perfect start to life. I told Sarah about this and as I was describing the lady I sucked my cheeks in to show that she was very thin like Loona had told me. Sarah laughed and said the description was perfect and that it was Loona's breeder who lived nearby.

Sarah and Loona have a great relationship which has built up over 13 years and it is wonderful to see a horse feeling so secure with her owner. Loona knows that she will be with Kate for life and is able to release her character and be herself. I carried on healing and Loona positioned herself in her "snoozy corner" and went quiet for a while. I worked my way through her body and she was like a sponge soaking in the healing energy. As I came round to her right pelvis, I heard someone shouting in my head, "sit back" they said, then a picture of a younger Sarah leaning forward in the saddle and not looking very confident at all came into my head. Sarah was having a lesson on Loona, the instructor shouted at Sarah and she sat back but she never let out the reins!! resulting in Loona being caught in the mouth. I told Sarah what Loona had shown me, her mum laughed and said that was the perfect description of her earlier lessons!

As I was healing Loona the word "fencing" came to me loud and clear, I asked Sarah to check her fencing, she said it had been repaired last weekend. I asked her to check it again in the area where Loona scratches her bottom, the posts are moving and Loona has her eye on the vegetable garden. Sarah burst out laughing and said I know exactly where that is, I told her that the neighbour has been digging vegetables and giving bits to Loona and being a bright spark Loona now knows there are carrot's in the ground!!!.

Loona became quiet again as I worked my way along her body until she showed me a picture of a bright pink bridle. I looked at Sarah and asked "you haven't got a pink bridle?" No" she replied, then her mum looked up and said " you have been talking about one, the one on Ebay." I passed on Loona's message that this was not a good idea! Loona's finishing comment was that "he" looking at the gelding had a rug that she didn't have! It was a light one, I thought at first it was a fly sheet. When I asked Sarah about this she knew exactly which one, it was the cotton cooler that he wears in his stable. I suggested that she should buy Loona one!!
It was one of the most amusing healings I have had and was wonderful to do and so good to see a horse being able to be herself and having such a sense of humour.

SUSIE

Susie is a 17 year old pony that I visited in Cornwall, Jo her owner described her as " lame as a coot!!"
I arrived and met Susie, a coloured pony who was indeed stiff and lame. As Susie walked towards me all her joints clicked, you actually heard her coming before you saw her. I introduced myself to Susie and asked if I could heal her, Susie came across as a woman of the world, full of confidence.
As I scanned over her body all her joints felt inflamed there were not many cool areas to be found. As I started healing Susie on her shoulder she started to communicate with me. She told me that she had been here before- Susie is an old soul and has lived before- she told me that she had been in the war. Not as a soldiers horse, she showed me pictures of her being a pack-pony carrying the cooking equipment for the soldiers. Susie had worked hard covering mile after mile she then gave me two words "love and respect". Susie was respected in her past life for the work that she did, she was important and part of a team. "Things are not like that this time around, watching horses and people there is a lack of respect." wise words from a wise mare.

Susie then returned to this life and the word 'matriarch' was given to me, when I got home I looked up the dictionary definition;
A woman who is the head of a family or tribe: in some cultures the mother proceeds to the status of a matriarch. An older woman who is powerful within a family or organization: a domineering matriarch.

This described Susie, she saw herself as the head of the family, she had taught them all to ride, from Mum to her daughter, and she had been a handful at times. She told me that she had not been easy she had thrown everything at them so they learnt! She showed me pictures of herself at a starting line it looked like a gymkhana and she was like a race horse, the excitement was too much and she could not stand still "I out ran them all" She said. Then I was shown a picture of one of the children on the ground and Susie a little way ahead looking back at them and waiting for them to pick themselves up and catch her up. I told Jo what I was being shown and she confirmed that Susie had been used as the children's' and her pony, she is now 18 and Jo told me that the children she had taught to ride had now become mums themselves, but Susie sees herself as head of the family!

I asked Susie about her body and what was wrong she told me some of the injuries are from her past life and that they are a reminder of the hard work that she did. Some are from now she showed me an incident in this lifetime where her side hit the ground with tremendous force. I could see her panicking and jumping what looked like a gate but misjudging the whole thing, catching her leg and landing on her side winded. Jo confirmed that this had been many years ago, Susie had jumped a gate after being frightened and caught herself, she hit the ground side on and was winded but otherwise ok.

I carried on healing Susie and she loved the energy soothing her joints, Susie is so happy with her life she knows who she is and what she is here to do, it is a joy to see. As I finished the healing with my hands on her head she stood there totally relaxed, licking and chewing.

CHARLIE

I had been asked by a lady called Pippa to visit her 29 year old pony, in recent weeks he had changed and she was very worried about him. When I arrived Charlie was outside his shelter in the field and Pippa took me across to him, when he saw us coming he became quite anxious. His eyes were big and he started pacing the fence as his energy became high, I hung back whilst Pippa caught him.

I slowly walked over talking to him and I could see him shaking, his eyes were bulging, it was all Pippa could do to hold him. Pippa his owner said that he has been like this more and more, with the farrier, or just having his rug changed, anything at all could set him off. I let Charlie get used to my energy and I asked him if I could work with him, Pippa took him into the shelter and he circled round and round. I stayed back and let Pippa settle him.

Pippa's baby then started crying and she had to check on him so I took the lead rein and walked with Charlie round and round the shelter. I worked on my breathing to bring my energy as low as I could and slowly he breathed deeper and calmed down. He came to a stop in the corner of the shelter and I quietly spoke to him and placed my hand on his neck, we were not going to take his rug off as it became too traumatic for him to have it back on. So I kept my hand on his neck, he accepted the healing and became calm and his head lowered as he relaxed.

I already knew that Charlie had not had a good start in life he had been a polo pony. As I was healing Charlie he relaxed enough to start communicating and showed me pictures of him shut in a stable spinning round and round, he was scared and anxious but the men just laughed at him. "They treated us tough to make us tough". Charlie had been very young barely three years old, there was no love and compassion but hard handling and mental cruelty. The treatment had made Charlie hard and caused him to switch his feelings off the same as a person would if they were abused and abused and no one listened. He learnt to be tough with them and they left him alone, every time someone used to try and get beneath that hard exterior he would shut down and buck, bolt, anything to be left alone again. This normally worked it kept them away, they never came back. Until Pippa "she kept coming back every day, I tried everything, I was dreadful to lead," he showed me a picture of a younger Pippa being dragged along by Charlie. "She tried to make me jump but I ran round the jump! and still she came back". Charlie started to lick and chew as the energy within started to flow and every so often his mind would wander and we would be back at the dreadful polo yard. I would gently bring him back to his life with Pippa and he would relax again.

Pippa joined us again and I carried on healing, I was drawn to his left eye, under my hand the area felt very hot. As I healed this area his head lowered and there was a feeling of relief throughout his body. As I was doing this Pippa started to tell me about her life with Charlie,15 years ago a very young Pippa had gone to a dealer's yard to buy a cob but she had felt so sorry for Charlie she had brought him instead. There life has been a challenge but she never gave up on him. She confirmed that for a long time Charlie had done all that he could to put her off. Nothing was easy but she had quietly persevered until they reached a mutual understanding and their life together had been fairly happy until recent months.

I explained to Pippa that Charlie in human terms is suffering with something similar to Dementia his mind/brain is not what it was and his behaviour has been erratic because he is slipping into the past and not staying in the present. When he is stressed his memory goes back to the bad days and when he is calm he is here in the now. This made sense to Pippa and she is going to get the vet out to give Charlie a check-up and ask his advice. Pippa contacted me and said the vet agreed, she is going to keep an eye on him and when the time is right have Charlie put to sleep so that he does not suffer.

POLO

I had a lovely healing with a horse called Polo and his owner Jill, Jill completed the paperwork and explained that her horse was well and happy but it would be nice for him to have a healing.

The relationship Jill and Polo have is beautiful, he is a character and has very sparky energy, he happily chomped on his hay and smelt my hands as I introduced myself. I felt him over and found his right side to have more energy blocks and issues than the left, this I showed Jill by dowsing over his body. Where the blocks were the crystals spiraled, as I moved them down his body they became calm.

I started on his left shoulder but he would not accept the healing, he kept nudging Jill's right shoulder and I asked her if she had a problem with her shoulder. She confirmed that she did and I explained that
Polo would not accept healing unless I placed one hand on her shoulder and gave her healing at the same time. She laughed and stood beside me, I placed one hand on her shoulder. I stood there with one hand on each of them, Polo rested his head on my shoulder as they both had healing. We stayed like this for some time all the other horses around us in the stables were also absorbing the healing and all were snoozing.

After a while the healing became too strong for Jill and she had to sit down, I carried on healing Polo. He started to communicate with me telling me that his mum, Jill, had been through a stressful time and when she is stressed so is he. Jill couldn't understand this and could not think of a time when she had been unduly stressed. I carried on healing and Polo said "bloody leg, the fence," none of this I understood until I spoke to Jill. She confirmed that she had had a fall whilst jumping and broke her leg. This also explained the comment about Jill being stressed; having your leg in plaster and a horse is not the easiest situation.

I carried on healing and got to the saddle area, there I felt heat and placed my hand on the area. A wave of sadness overcame me as I felt his emotion over the loss of his friend, I knew that he had changed yards in recent months and felt very strongly that this friend had been there. Jill confirmed that he had a special friend at the old yard but he had moved somewhere else before Polo had left. I stayed with the emotion and Polo showed me how he felt at weaning, also when another horse had died. The feeling was the same, huge loss and sadness from never being able to say goodbye. I carried on healing him telling him I understood, he relaxed, his head became lower his eyes heavy as he licked and chewed and then yawned as he let the emotion go and the energy flow. I told Jill what I had been shown and explained that horses feel the same as us, a loss of a friend can be as hard as coping with a death. If it happens again tell Polo why it needs to happen and let him say goodbye, I told Jill that she will feel a bit silly doing this but it would help Polo.

After a break I changed to his right side which was totally different, the emotion here was anger from fear. I placed my hands on his shoulder and asked him what it was, I had a man's voice come into my head, definitely Irish. Polo was one of many in a field, there was a lot of commotion as the tractor brought the big bale of hay in. The man was shouting from the tractor and there was panic and confusion coming from Polo. From what I was shown the horses were kept and fed like cows, the man was a hard man and Polo was scared of him. He showed me pictures of the man rounding up the horses, if you went the wrong way you were beaten with a stick. Once the horses were in the barn people would come to look at them, some were separated and made to canter and gallop. From what he was showing me it was people coming and looking to buy. I carried on healing the shoulder area until Polo's energy had come down and he was relaxed and licking and chewing, the heat started to disappear and the memory healed.

As I moved down through his body, I placed my hands just before the pelvis where there was heat, Polo
lifted up his hind leg, not to kick but to warn, so I backed away and healed from a distance. Polo circled the box and I stayed with him until he was happy for me to touch him. He relaxed and accepted the healing on his back, as I was healing, the shoulder muscle trembled as the energy traveled through the body. I asked him what it was all about; he showed me a scene I had been shown before of horses being handled by the men and let's just say not everything was done by a vet or farrier. Polo became very quiet as I healed the area and relaxed until he yawned and yawned and Jill joined in as she picked up on the healing energy.

I placed my hands in front of his head and he lowered his head until his lips were touching my hand and I had my fingers on his gums, I felt pain and healed the area. Then I placed my hand on his head and we stayed like this for quite a while as the energy within his body rebalanced and he became totally relaxed.

Afterwards I talked to Jill about what Polo had shown me and she confirmed he had come from Ireland and had not had a good start. When he arrived she asked the vet to check him over and it was discovered that his teeth had never been rasped and his gums and cheeks were very sore. Polo has not had the best start in life but Jill has made his life happy and a beautiful partnership has blossomed.

JOSH

I went to see a stunning stallion called Josh; he has a very large character with lots of presence, he is a big stallion, black and white in colour. I introduced myself and slowly scanned him over, as I was doing this I could feel that Julie his owner was not totally convinced about my work. I spoke to Josh and told him what I felt, I asked him to give me something that would change Julie's opinion and enable us all to relax. He started communicating telling me he came from Holland, when he told me this I wasn't sure if he was winding me up, I could feel that he had a huge sense of humour! I told Julie his owner and she nodded her head and said" yes he did", I told her he was showing me big posh gates and green fields and the area was very flat. I have only been to Suffolk a couple of times but when I went I was amazed how flat it was and this was the same.

Josh then showed me a very tall thin man with a heavily lined face, he was very stern and he showed me that they were fed, watered, worked, and that there was no affection or emotion shown. By work I mean that he covered lots of mares from a very young age, he liked his work and the ladies but there had been one who kicked him badly. I told Julie about this and she confirmed that he had covered lots of mares and he had had a leg injury from one, but it did not put him off. I felt that during this time he would have been stabled all the time and not let out to graze, I asked him about this, he showed me grass and took my hands to his tummy. As I placed my hands on the area I could see the colour red and felt that later on when he had been allowed out the grass had upset the balance of his gut because he was not used to it.

I carried on healing and Josh then told me he came over to the UK via Ireland! I asked him why? he told me it was for a viewing. I told Julie this but we have no idea if he was telling porkies as he is a bit of a comedian. As a result of this he has had some tough handling, to some his humour came over as disobedience and he paid the price. But if you embraced his energy and character and laughed with him you could fly, he showed me pictures of him with springs under his hooves. Julie confirmed this she said that if you relaxed and absorbed his movement and let him flow it is amazing, he has natural elevation. When I placed my hand around the wither he showed me that there had been saddle problems which have caused pressure and pain.

I changed to his left side and was instantly drawn to his lower leg, he showed me pictures of the leg bandaged. I told Julie about this as I was healing the area, she confirmed that they are having problems with the leg and that he had just completed box rest with the leg bandaged. The word arthritis came to me which is possible in a horse of his age and the vets are aware of the problem. The problem with the leg is causing problems with his shoulder and up to his wither this would make his stride uneven and short. He stood still and absorbed the healing energy in the leg and shoulder and as I was doing this Josh showed me a picture of himself, he was much thinner than he is now and in poor condition. His energy was also incredibly flat and I would not have recognised him, I described what I was seeing to Julie who confirmed that he had been in a poor condition when she had got him. His previous owner could not cope with him and I guessed that he was kept thin to try and keep him quieter to handle. He had also spent a lot of time tied up in the stable because he box walked. I later understood that this was over a period of six years. Can you imagine being tied up all the time unless you were being worked, surely the right thing would have been to find out why he box walks and sort the problem. As a result of this Julie has had to introduce Josh to more freedom, you would think this is something he would have embraced, but, it had the opposite effect. He panics if he is not tied up, if Julie is on the yard he is calm and will be like any other horse in the stable, but if she leaves, any noise or people coming and going upsets him. They have found a way of coping, when Julie is around he is turned out in the field or in his stable. When he is in and she leaves him he has a long rope attached to his haynet and he stands and eats happily, it completely calms him down and gives him security. They have now got to a stage where he can be left untied at night as long as Julie is first on the yard in the morning.

Josh took in lots of healing; his final words to me were that he disliked hacking and the rain, Julie confirmed that hacking was not one of his favourite activities and asked me to tell him that it was something that needed to be done. I did pass the message on but do not feel that it will become his favourite past time. At the end of the healing Josh reminded Julie of when he has been sedated! Head nearly on the ground and half asleep, totally relaxed. As I finished he brought his head up and did the most beautiful stretch from poll to tail releasing all tension within.

The next week I was treating another horse on the yard and I went to say hello to Josh, he was tied to his haynet. I could see straight away that this was like a security blanket to him, he had spent so long tied up over his life that it is what he is used to, when the yard is busy and Julie is not there he feels safe and secure. It was amazing to see how contented he was, knowing that if he was not tied up he would be stressed and box walking. Sometimes when we take on horses that have been through hard handling we have to find ways to keep them happy, to some tied up is not the best option. But if you saw Josh you would soon realise that this was right for him. It may not be right for other horses but we have to remember that they are all individuals like you and I.

A DOUBLE HEALING

I had the wonderful pleasure of healing two beautiful horses belonging to Lyn, the first was a 24 year old pony who had been with Lyn since he was 6, he had been her first pony. At the moment Jack has laminitis and is quite uncomfortable and is being treated by the vet.

What was so lovely about Jack was how contented and happy this old pony was about his life. Jack is one of a few who has stayed in one home for many years, as a result of this he is secure in where he is and who he is. I gave him a lovely healing on his old body, he showed me pictures of a child on him, riding in just a head collar, a young girl who was wearing shorts and wellies. It was a beautiful picture and I asked Lyn about this "that would have been when I was very young, having the farm here I would go out and jump on Jack and we would go for long rides around the farm. Just as we were, no posh clothes and tack or preplanning just me and my Jack."

Jack's healing was beautiful he has had a happy life and accepted healing in all his old joints; he is a lovely and very lucky pony...........

Lyn's other horse was a big beautiful 10 year old mare who Lyn had bred on the farm. I introduced myself to Lucy and started scanning her over; I felt heat in her right shoulder but nothing too bad, I then went round to the left. This side was completely different, had Lyn been trying to ride her she would have found Lucy very stiff on the right rein. The energy through this side of the body was completely blocked; I mentioned this to Lyn who said that before Lucy had been turned away for the winter she had been very difficult to lunge on the right rein. As I was working with Lucy her mum was watching from the adjoining stable.

Again Lucy had only ever known the one home and what a huge difference it makes, she is a happy, secure and contented mare. I started healing her, the neck and shoulder became so hot that I asked Lyn to place her hand there and see if she could feel the heat "Oh yes" she said "it's really hot". I worked on clearing the block and the mare started to talk to me. As she was talking she kept nudging Lyn telling me how stressed Lyn had been and that she needed to relax. Things have not been good for a while and she is not herself she said. I kept my hand on Lucy and turned to Lyn and told her that the mare was worried about her and that she is storing a lot of emotion. Lyn looked at me and her eyes filled with tears as she told me about the problems in her life. As she was doing this and the emotion was released Lucy licked and chewed and relaxed releasing the energy held in her body. I carried on working with Lucy down through her left side and then she asked me to include Lyn in the healing. I said if I was to do this Lucy had to show me where Lyn needed healing. Lucy reached out with her head and pulled at Lyn's shoulder and I explained what Lucy wanted to happen. Lyn looked slightly surprised but agreed so I placed my hand on Lucy and the other on Lyn. The healing energy started to work it's magic, Lucy drifted off into a contented doze and rested her head on my shoulder and Lyn could feel the energy coming into her body and spreading up into her ear. She later explained that she had been suffering with an ear infection, the healing was very intense and after a while Lyn needed to sit down, I carried on working on Lucy making sure everything was cleared and the energy flowing. The horse licked and chewed and yawned, releasing all the worry that she had been holding about her owner.

I explained to Lyn that the close relationship she has with Lucy means that Lucy picks up on everything going on inside her body, you may look like you are coping to the outside world but inside the energy will be a lot different, inside you have stored the sadness and unhappiness and Lucy worries about this. Now that they have had the joint healing I hope that both of them will be clear and their energy running smoothly. Always remember that you can put on a happy face to everyone else but your horse knows what is really going on and is affected by our inner energy.

It was so lovely to meet these happy horses who care so much for their owner, as she said; it may not be the Hilton, the horses live in a converted cow barn but the horses are by far some of the happiest that I have met. Just goes to show the outside cover of posh stables doesn't matter to the horse but the quality of life and partnership does..........................

TOM

I went out to visit Tom who I knew was an x-racehorse, I went expecting the normal heartache that I had felt before when healing race horses. But, I had the most beautiful healing with a chap who let me into his soul. When this happens there are no words to describe the experience.

Tom's owner Sue had asked me to visit because of Tom's dreadful separation anxiety. He hated being taken away from his friends and this was making life difficult. When I arrived Tom was in the yard with his herd, as we approached, the horses wandered to the field gate and Tom went to join them.

Sue put Tom's head collar on, we kept his friends in the yard with him and I started the healing. As I stood there waiting for him to get used to my energy the first thing he said to me was "I don't do people" I acknowledged this and asked him if I could touch him, I touched his shoulder and started scanning over his body with my hand. As I was doing this he told me "I was a winner," I was not surprised, his body felt good under my hand. When race horses are successful they receive the best treatment all strains are looked after, so that they can perform to the best of their ability and in turn earn their owner money. When race horses are not successful they can receive harsh treatment, everyone wants their horse to win so the pressure can be immense. When they don't win the odd knock and strain is not dealt with but left. So they have old injuries and also a lot of stress held within from the mental pressure and physical strain from trying their best. Life had been good to Tom and he showed me one person who had been very important to him, it was a female and from what I was being shown I would say it was his groom. There had been no stress and he had the best life ever. He did not give me any more information on this special person and I carried on with the healing.

He told me he hated being on his own and showed me a picture of him when he was very young, but I didn't feel that he was showing me the full picture. The other horses on the yard started to move away and he became stressed but I reached inside and asked him to stay with me. He did, he became very quiet and his eyes half closed and we met soul to soul. Tom then gave me his story, life had been good and he had felt that he was one of the lucky ones; he had been in a very good place. He had been well looked after and always had a full belly he had not known hunger like some of the horses I meet. But then it had all changed, he did not understand what happened, slowly everyone horse and human in his life went and he blamed himself. He had been used to being top of the tree and running on adrenaline but all of a sudden life was empty. This is why he clung to the herd natural instinct, he released a lot of stress and I felt his huge sadness within me as I cried his tears and when I looked up so did everyone who was watching. I told him that it will be ok he is now in a forever home and he will not be left. Then one of the other horses who had stayed nearby came over and joined the healing he licked my hand and said" I will look after him." The three of us continued the healing and words cannot describe how it all felt-so special.

At the end of the healing Sue filled in the missing pieces, Tom had been a special racehorse he had been in a small racing yard for 12 years and had been very successful and well looked after. He had a constant groom he loved, and then all of a sudden the yard closed and he was sent to the auction. His groom bided and managed to buy him at the auction but unfortunately could not afford to keep him and he ended up at another yard, this is where Sue found him. But the memories had gone deep and he panicked about what might happen next but he felt safe with the herd it was natural instinct.

I have told him that the people at his new home love him and he needs to give them a chance he hugged my leg and we were one. When the healing finished he was quiet and happy to stay on the yard even though the others had gone, we hope this will continue.

JK

A lovely horse I treated was the handsome JK, I had been called to treat Jk to see what he had to say about life. He is a beautiful horse with a huge heart, I introduced myself and scanned JK over on the left, he told me his knee ached and circulation was slow resulting in the leg being cold. He told me he had a lot to teach his owner Jane and she agreed confirming that he is her school master.

I felt down beside his wither and he told me there was damage from a saddle a long time ago, along the back towards the pelvis there is arthritis, this is how he spoke very straight to the point. He hates being cold and needs to be kept warm. I then changed to his right side and felt tremendous heat in his neck which went down into his shoulder. As I was healing, the heat intensified and I asked Jane to run her hand down his neck so that she could feel where the problem is and keep an eye on it. I carried on healing and he showed me how he had been tied up in a confined space. I thought he was in a lorry or trailer and the feeling he gave me was panic, he didn't want to go in. Then the picture became clearer and it looked like a crate that horses were flown in. I spoke to Jane about what I was seeing, and asked her if JK had ever been in a plane. She said that he had come from Ireland but was not sure how he had got to the UK.

I carried on healing JK and he started to bite me and became quite aggressive. His owner became quite concerned and asked if I wanted her to hold him, I declined the offer I wanted to go deeper and find the reason for the anger. I carried on healing down his right side and we circled the box a few times. I asked him what was going on, what was making him angry. He then gave me the name "Bojangle" I told Jane but this didn't mean anything to her, so I went deeper. Jk then stood still and gave me the song, "Mr Bo jangle", along with this I saw a lovely stable block and an old groom with a rolled cigarette in his mouth grooming JK, his coat shone like a mirror. The feeling that came through with this was of relaxation and happiness and all the time the song Mr Bo jangles playing, the lyrics, ragged shirt and worn out shoes described the groom that I could see and those horses loved him. JK then showed me a long strip of grass which must have been a racetrack and he galloped, but said "not fast enough".

That seems to be when the journey started, he was sold and transported but he didn't want to leave Bojangle-the groom. I stood with his head in my hands and went deep into his soul the song still playing and his words of why? why were we parted? I apologised to him on behalf of mankind and said that he would be together again with Mr Bojangle in another world one day. The sadness I felt I can not describe and I let his emotion wash through me and cried his tears, after a while he licked and chewed and then yawned and yawned as the anxiety left his body. Slowly he came back to the present and I looked up at Jane who was lost for words and very emotional. The song Mr Bojangle had been played at the racing stables and I suggested to Jane that she may like to do this now. Jk is now happy and very spoilt as he deserves to be, the memory he held for so many years has now been aired.

You know, sometimes I question my sanity, not often but a remark will reach me the body will be tired and the bank balance will not balance! and I think what is it like to be normal? To not hear the voice, see horses as some people do just to use and then pass on. Then I am sent a special horse to take me on a journey a very special journey, ok very emotional, but it brings home my message to people; horses think, feel every emotion that we do. They feel huge love for good people in their life and when for what ever reason they are no longer together the scars go deep. I drove home playing Mr Bo jangles crying the tears of all horses that are not understood and gave thanks that I had been chosen to help the horse.

If you have the song Mr Bo jangles sit back and play it and listen to the words, see the stables, the relaxed loved horse and old Bo Jangles in his ragged shirt and worn shoes polishing their coats until they shone.

OLLY

On my travels I am lucky to visit beautiful parts of the country, one of my favorites is Bodmin, I had been booked to visit a horse called Olly. I arrived at a wonderful old farm and met Clare, Olly's owner, I knew that Clare had lost her nerve riding and she wanted to know how Olly felt about everything. I also knew that Olly had had a fall out hacking with Clare's mum and this was making Clare worry even more.

I introduced myself to Olly and stood for a while chatting with Clare and let Olly get used to my energy, I then asked him if I could heal him. I put my hand on his shoulder and he was happy so I started to scan his body. Under my hand his body felt good, there were no huge areas of heat but he was not as happy as I felt he should be. His energy was not flowing and it was like there was a black cloud over him, he chatted to me straight away, he told me he was confused about Clare not riding him and was worried that this would mean a new home. Clare assured me that Olly would be going nowhere, which I told him. He thought about this for a moment and said he couldn't however understand why Clare was anxious all the time he also said she had a bad neck and shoulders because of this anxiety. I turned to Clare and told her that Olly is picking up on her stress and also that this is making her neck and shoulders ache.

Olly wanted me to put my hand on Clare's shoulder which I did; I stood there with one hand on Clare and the other on Olly. Whilst doing this I asked him about the fall, he showed me pictures of him walking, his feet were long and his shoes shiny there was nothing to grip with. I saw him going down a hill and being frightened at something in the hedge and as he shied he lost his grip on the road resulting in not only Olly falling but also Clare's Mum. He then told me about the lady with the bad hip who rode him, he felt that she did not move evenly in the saddle. I mentioned this to Clare who confirmed that her Mum had been riding Olly and that she had a bad hip
.
He then started talking about Clare again, he showed me a picture of him with all his tack on and Clare leading him. "Take me for walks" he said, I told Clare that Olly wanted her to lead him out onto the moors, if she felt happy, to get on, if she felt anxious at all to get off and walk a while. Clare was amazed because this was something that she had been thinking about doing. I explained that Olly was really missing their time together; he then gave me the nursery rhyme Humpty Dumpty and said that if she was anxious start singing the rhyme and it would relax her. He also said that I had to tell her about the breathing to keep her relaxed! I explained to Clare about the importance of breathing and how she could not only relax herself but also Olly if she worked on her breathing.

I carried on healing Olly and he relaxed as he accepted the healing energy, he became quiet for a while then he started to communicate again. He told me that Clare had become very stressed and anxious, "part of the reason she is stressed is because of her tummy" he said and gently reached out and touched her tummy with his nose. I told Clare what Olly was saying and she became emotional and let her tears fall, She confirmed that there are problems that were worrying her and she was having lots of tests at the moment. Olly interrupted and told me to tell Clare that she would be ok. Clare was amazed with the comments from Olly and how much he knew, I explained that horses read our inner energy and read our thoughts and know far more about us than people think!!

I finished the healing on Olly and he relaxed and licked and chewed and then let out the biggest yawns ever. Olly and Jane have a wonderful relationship and she needs to start trusting him so that they can enjoy their rides out on Bodmin.

COPPER

Copper is a beautiful blond Haflinger, he belongs to a lady called Yvon and is kept on a hill on top of Dartmoor. I love visiting not only to see Yvon and the horses but also to feel the energy of the moors, it clears away the cobwebs. I first went at the beginning of 2013, Yvon had heard about me and wanted to see if I could help Copper. He had recently had a dreadful time with laminitis and she was hoping that healing would help him.

During this visit Copper had a lot to say, he told me about his equine friend who had died and the mischief they used to get up to. He then became quiet as I focused on his healing, his front legs were very uncomfortable and his hooves felt hot. He was finding it difficult to walk and had been fenced into a small area to restrict his grazing, he did not think very much of this and asked that his words be passed on. Yvon laughed and said "he will have to get used to it, it's for his own good." During the healing Copper released all anxiety from his body by yawning and yawning. After this he made a good recovery although his hooves will never be right and he continued to do well until the Autumn when I received another call asking for a visit.

When I arrived Copper was lying down and in a lot of pain his pedal bones had started to rotate and standing was difficult. The vet had been and x-rays taken and Yvon's farrier was now visiting every two weeks to try and help.

I walked up the field to Copper and got down on my knees, I asked Copper if he would like some healing, although in pain he was in good spirits and was as pleased to see me as normal. He asked that I undo his neck cover and let his blond mane blow in the breeze. Yvon laughed and said "he always seems so proud of his mane". Copper was in a lot of discomfort and I gave him healing until he was relaxed and I hoped that it had helped him, when I left I was very worried about him.

Three months later I had a call from Yvon asking me to go and see her and Copper. I arrived to find Copper up and walking around, he was back to his cheeky self, he was standing and walking around with the other horses. I asked him if he would like to have some healing and I placed my hand on his shoulder. He started communicating saying "you are not a natural like me". I looked at him and he shook his mane, I laughed and told Yvon what he had said. Copper then turned and took my hat off and trotted across the field, revealing my dark roots to the world! We couldn't stop laughing, I was so pleased to see Copper well and moving around, that I forgave his comment about my hair colour.

When I caught up with him and he stood still Copper stood and welcomed the healing energy into his body. He told me that he was ok, he told me that the vet didn't know what he was doing and told me to tell Yvon to listen to the farrier. "He knew what he was doing," as a result Copper was much more comfortable. He showed me cushions under his hoofs, I told Yvon this and she said that she would put his padded boots back on! I carried on healing Copper, he took as much as he needed I then went to see the other horses.

I last saw Jake when he was grieving for a horse that had passed to spirit, he had taken me across the field so that we were on our own. I then gave him the most beautiful healing to help him come to terms with the loss of his equine friend. This time he was much happier as I offered him healing, he stood still and showed me a picture of Yvon on the ground not looking very well. I asked her about this and she explained that she had been very poorly and often had to sit down as she felt so ill. I told her that the horses had noticed and that she needed to ask for help and not try and do it all on her own.

Yvon has a wonderful relationship with her horses and they all love and care for each other. Yvon is very much part of the herd and there is respect all round for both horse and people.

8

THE PARTING

October 2013 I had my beautiful Grace put to sleep, as I stood in the field with our other horses crying my tears. The wind suddenly blew and Graces words came to me;

"I'll be the flowers in the Spring, the wind in your face and the stars in the sky.

I will never leave you, I will walk by your side the voice of the horse is now one as "The Horses Voice"

Whenever and for whatever reason it happens it is never easy having to put your horse to sleep, whether it is through injury, illness or old age the thought of having to make that dreadful decision is one we put to the back of our minds until it has to be faced. People ask my views on injection or gun, for me it is injection but it is a very personal choice. What is right for one person may not be for the other.

Death to a lot of people is a disturbing thought which scares them and obviously upsets them; I see death as going home. Going back to spirit from where we have all come, when horses need to be put to sleep for whatever reason I see them being out of pain and retreating to a beautiful place. A place where no harm can come to them, I am often asked about the best way for the other horses to be treated when a friend dies. I always recommend allowing the horses friend to spend time with the body, you will normally find they will sniff their friend and sense the energy and life force has gone. Some will smell them for a long while; some will touch them with their hoof. It has been known for the friend to let out a loud whinny and some a deep sigh, they may start to graze around the body or walk around their friend and when they are happy all energy has gone they walk away. This process can never be rushed, you have to remember the friend will be grieving and will have to mourn the loss of their friend. Do not be surprised if the horse friend over the next few days or even weeks becomes quiet and withdrawn he is grieving and will come back to you when he is ready.

I have been asked to give healing to horses as they pass, this I am happy to do I stand at the horses head with my hand on their shoulder or neck and tell them what is about to happen. The vet carries out the injection and I am sending healing and love to the horse, I carry on doing this until they have sunk to the floor and the heart stops. I say a healing prayer, asking for my guides to help the spirit of the horse to pass over to the other side. I see the energy of the horse leave the body, they start to pass over and always look back at what they had been. All pain has gone and the old look young and agile again. Once they have looked I tell them it is ok and they move away to a golden light.

Although a very sad experience for me it is also beautiful that I am able to do this. Never be afraid of death, the spirit lives on, all that is left is the skin and bones that have carried the body during its life here on earth.

One horse I was with on passing was a Welsh cob called Crowe who had been given to me when my children were very young. I wanted a horse that I could hack out on and my friend had given me Crowe, she was in her twenties and hadn't had the best of lives. But for the few years she was with me she was treated like a Queen, kept at home and she was my salvation from baby sick and nappies! We would go out for gentle hacks and relaxation both of us asking nothing from each other apart from companionship and relaxation.

One morning I went out to Crowe to turn her out and she was very quiet I put on her head collar and she nudged her leg showing me there was something wrong. I asked her to move but it was obvious that she could not walk. The vet was called and examined her, we agreed to give her bute and see if the shoulder got better. Crowe was very arthritic and I knew that something had gone in the shoulder and my intuition told me it would not come right, but I had to give it a chance.

After a couple of days Crowe was comfortable eating and drinking but was not moving any better, that evening I went out and checked her. The bute was wearing off and the discomfort was there for all to see, I stroked her head and she looked me in the eye and told me the time had come. I spent some time with her breathing in her smell and feeling the warmth under my hand, it was with a heavy heart I returned to the house and called the vet. Tom arrived and said unfortunately he could not turn back time and Crowe was an old lady, I stayed with Crowe whilst he administered the injection and I watched the life leave my best friend.

I knew that Crowe was now pain free and in a beautiful place but I missed her so much and I gave myself time to mourn. Never under estimate how much the death of your equine friend will affect you, tears need to be cried and the heart needs to heal. In time life moves on but if you think of them they come to you and are always near.

STELLA

I arrived at my yard one morning to find Stella showing signs of colic. I phoned Jill Stella's owner and the vet, they both arrived and the vet examined Stella. He gave her pain relief and after the examination confirmed that her intestine was blocked and tried to tube her to put fluid into her stomach to see if it could be flushed through. After a period of time it became apparent that nothing had changed and he gave more medicine and pain relief. Stella was more comfortable for a while and I managed to have a chat with Jill as to what she wanted to do.

Obviously Jill wanted Stella to recover and be well, but, there was also a chance the decision would have to be made to put Stella to sleep and I needed to talk to her about this. Stella was 25 and had a lovely life with Jill, she was not insured and Jill confirmed she would not have her operated on.

After a couple of hours it became clear that Stella was again in horrific pain and the vet came back, he again administered pain relief and again went saying he would return in two hours. This went on until mid-afternoon when Stella was in so much pain she didn't know what to do with herself; she was circling her box and was lathered with sweat. The vet arrived and again pain relief was given and Jill was told to see what happens and he would return in another two hours.

By now Jill was beside herself and very upset, the vet would not advise her and I could see Stella walking round and round her box. The vet went to go again and I stopped him, I did not feel this was right something had to be done one way or the other. The vet would not and was not allowed to tell Jill to put Stella to sleep, he was administering pain relief but the problem was still there. Stella had a blockage and she was now very ill.

I had a word with Jill who was very upset, I told her that a decision had to be made, the vet had told her that Stella needed to be operated on. For Jill it was like telling the Doctor to switch off the Life Support Machine, Stella had been her friend and companion for over twenty years, but, she made the decision and the vet prepared the injection. I stood with Jill and Stella while she whispered her goodbyes. Jill asked me to be with Stella, she stayed for the first part of the injection and saw that Stella was not in pain and very sleepy. She then left the yard and I stayed with Stella as the final dose was given, Stella fell to the ground and her heart stopped beating, the limbs twitched as the energy left her body. I kept my hand on Stella talking to her and giving her healing, I then saw her leave her body a young beautiful horse in full glory she looked at me and I told her it was ok to go and into the golden light she went. Jill then returned to the barn and said her goodbyes and I made the arrangements for Stella's body to be collected.

IVAN

I was called by Colleen a client of mine who owned two heavy cobs which were used for riding and driving. When I answered the phone Colleen was very upset and told me that DJ one of the cobs had been put to sleep as a result of colic. She was very worried about Ivan who although had other horses for company was withdrawn and not himself.

I went out to Ivan the next day and after hugging Colleen who was obviously very upset and grieving I went into the field. Normally Ivan would come to meet us but this time we had to walk to him. I stroked his head and felt his anguish; I gave him healing but felt a barrier between us. Ivan needed to move away from Colleen so I took the rope and Ivan led me to the edge of the field away from the others. He stopped at the hedge and turned and looked at me eye to eye. He had questions; "where had he gone? Why had he not come back?" Ivan was sad, lost and confused, DJ had been taken to the vet and died whilst being operated on so Ivan had not seen his body or said goodbye. I explained to Ivan what had happened and gave him healing as I healed him, I felt his emotion and cried his tears for him. I told him that he was in charge now and had to guide the young horse and carry on with DJ's work. He sighed and yawned and yawned as the anxiety and grief left his body, I told Ivan that in time DJ would be back and he would see his spirit.

I have since visited Ivan who spent a period of time grieving, when I next saw him he was carrying on with DJ's work guiding the youngster. As I healed him he said "you were right Lainey, he has come back and I do see him". I agreed with him and smiled as I saw DJ's energy bouncing around us……………

I am not going to write lots about the passing as my aim is not to upset you; it is a fact of life and needs to be thought about. These beautiful animals come into our life and form a huge bond but unfortunately, where there is life there is death. The movement of time is something no one can change but when the time comes remember your friend will never really leave you, their spirit will visit and hopefully if you are lucky you will be aware of this. You will feel their energy or perhaps feel a movement near you always believe that they are there, thank them and they will keep coming back.

9

THE SALES

Unfortunately we are living in times where there are no limits to breeding or importing horses. Our little Island is full to the seams and there are not enough homes for them all. The sanctuaries are full and there seems nothing can be done.

In the Autumn of 2012 I was asked by my guides to visit the sales, this was not something I wanted to do as the suffering the ponies go through is immense. But there was also a part of me that wanted to see for myself exactly what goes on, this was my day………………….

I had a sleepless night and embraced the day with terror, sickness and sadness, I knew that this day would push me further than I have been pushed before. I picked up a friend and off we went. When we arrived there were not too many people there and I thought perhaps there would not be too many horses. Within half an hour the lorries and cars were arriving and the cries of the horses could be heard, they ripped at my heart as I heard them call. Yet looking around me people were going around the stalls, the whole atmosphere was like a carnival. Families were there for a day out there was much laughter and the sounds of a social occasion.

We started to walk around the pens which are small wooden constructions, literally penning the horse in. There is no access to water and they can stay there from dawn to dusk. The foals, some so small they should not have been taken from their mum's, there had been no gradual weaning for them. We saw twelve foals in a pen ages ranging from 3 to 7 months. They were all panicking trying to get into the corner, scared, frightened, calling out in their high pitched whinnies but no replies coming. One foal was so angry it wanted to kill the world, lashing out at anything that came near; the others had trouble getting away and suffered the kicks. Nobody seemed affected by what they were watching and I went and found the RSPCA man who said that they put so many in together so that if they do kick they can't get a full swing. There were empty pens in that row they did not need to have so many together.

I walked past all the horses offering my love and saying sorry, they looked at me eye to eye with fear, anger, pain and so much sadness in their bodies, they were crying out for help, sensory overload for them and me. Some had shut down they could no longer cope and the shutters had closed, the body numb and the mind blank. One horse was on his own in an area so small he could hardly turnaround, he was so stressed he was grinding his teeth and weaving from side to side.

As I walked around I was picking up everything from the horses, yet as I looked around I could see that nobody else was seeing or feeling it, the people were immune to feeling the horses pain. The foals and horses are looking out at a sea of unfeeling flesh, poking, prodding and some laughing when they see the horse distressed, not realising or caring what the horses are going through. Is this why society is in such a bad place? Have people really become so far removed from their feelings that they no longer feel anything? Our eyes see the distress but as people we seem to have a mechanism to ignore it, blank it out and carry on with our lives.

There were television people there with a well known presenter telling people about the lovely ponies, reading from the sales book, laughing and joking. They could not see that what they are filming is cruelty, depression, sadness and so much fear I could taste it. I approached the camera man and told him to film outside in the trees where there were more horses and other animals. He didn't seem too keen on this, filming in the adjoining area would have been completely different. Puppies were being sold from the back of vans, barely old enough to walk but if you were prepared to buy then yours for £100 cash! I watched one man open the back of his van and cowering inside were five

Dalmatian puppies all for sale.

In the trees you have the travelers and their horses, the atmosphere in this area was quite threatening, I watched nine horses being pulled out of a cattle trailer, it had been towed by a short wheel base 4x4 completely overloaded. They had just driven past 2 police officers who were checking vehicles! The state of these horses was unbelievable, so thin, depressed and with dull coats. I have never witnessed anything like it before, Shetland foals being carried by their tails, unhandled foals desperately trying to escape as the home made rope halters dug into their skin. Men with big ego's using such force on the horses a well-aimed kick would make them look big and hard, wouldn't it?

I have never wanted to lash out at so many people in all my life. I have never seen such sad depressed horses in one place. They had switched off and shutdown, they are taken to the sales and tied to a tree, all for sale. No water or hay and left all day and if they are very lucky a kind person will buy them and nurse them back to health and give them a life they deserve. As I walked through the woods I could feel the horses eyes boring into me calling for help, so scared they were at breaking point. All of these horses are for sale, 95% of them are in such poor condition they are RSPCA cases. But as I have found in the past, unless the horse is in danger of dying by which time it is to late the RSPCA can not get involved.

These people are tough you do not approach them, so I went over to talk to the police. I asked them why they had not stopped the truck which was not only overloaded with horses but also people. "We do not have the resources to look in the vehicles and trailers, we are checking the lights. We have nothing here to weigh the vehicles" I pointed out that they could see in the car and trailer and it was blindingly obvious that the trailer and car were overloaded, they were a danger to other road users, not to

mention animal welfare. "This is not our department" she replied "we cannot weigh the trailers and we don't have room to pull them over" I pointed out that behind them was the whole of the New
Forest how much room did they need. "We have not been told to check the inside of trailers" I asked about common sense but it seems they are not allowed to use this.

Later on that day I stood and watched a horse being trotted very fast up and down the center of the road, it was a "trotter" attached to a buggy with a large man sat in it. Vehicles had to get out of the way to avoid them as the horse was shown to perspective buyers. The horse was panicking and in distress its head and neck locked as the man pulled with all his weight against the reins. Up and down they went and yet again the police stood and watched. The horse is trotted at fast speed, some of them as young as two years old and still growing. The trotting damages their joints and their mouths are often bleeding as force is used on the reins. The horse is scared, head high, eyes bulging, panicking as the drivers of the buggies pull on the reins with all of their body weight. I turned and looked at the police, they stood there watching and doing nothing.

I returned to the sale area and took a deep breath, I had to have a drink as I was picking up on the horses need of water. I went to the sale area where you bid for the horses, I could not go near the ring, but stood outside filming where they came out. It is now law that all foals must be micro-chipped, so on leaving the ring they are herded into a crush; a crush has metal sides that move in to pin the horse so that they can't move. The noise can be deafening as they panic and try to get out. The sides move in and pin them whilst the vet inserts the chip into their neck. The stress that these youngsters go through during this process is huge and yet there are people sat on the rails watching and not feeling the pain. This is the hardest thing for me to understand that people do not feel what I feel, have they really turned their hearts to lead that they cannot at least see?

One mare came out of the sale ring and her foal was herded into the crush, she panicked and became very distressed about having her foal separated from her. She could hear it calling and banging around and could do nothing to help. It is the same as you or I would feel if your child was taken from you and physically abused, you could hear it all but you could not get to them. Whilst witnessing this I overheard a conversation between two men one who was working there. He had put it to the board that all foals should be weaned before they are sold to reduce the stress of mare and foal. At last someone who could see and feel it, he said that the board didn't think much of the idea but he would keep on until they listened. One person among so many I saw that day that showed compassion for the horses.

For others, no one wants to know how the horses felt at the sales, it is easier for them all to believe that animals do not feel, they do not have emotions. But they do and going through the auctions can damage them for life. For some it is the end of their life, they are herded into the meat lorry and driven to the abattoirs where their life is ended. In some ways this is a release from the cruelty inflicted by mankind for once the bullet is shot and the brain stops the heart ceases to beat and then the spirit is free. I believe in Spirit, there is no pain and they are safe which is more than they were in their short lives on earth. For others they are "rescued" by well meaning people, but this is not always as wonderful as it sounds. People are taking in a wild animal, most have hardly had any handling and they are scared and confused. When the young wild pony reaches what is to be their home great care and understanding is needed. For the foals it is often easier to earn their trust than the older horses,

It is time to listen, it's time to start caring and if you start by what you see at the sales then maybe... you will care about life, and others around you and then the world will become a better place.

So for me there are no words to describe how I felt about the sales I was numb and It took a few days to sort out my head and send as much love and healing to the horses in the world, for that day at the sales was just one sale in a small place there are many more......................

10
THE LAST CHAPTER

Well, the last chapter of the first book! Never thought I would get this far.

It has been a long spiritual journey and one that continues and unfolds day by day. Horses Voice is growing, we have over twenty students now all learning about themselves and eventually learning to heal and connect with horses. We have set up the Lafayette Equine Healing and Communication Society where all can learn about this beautiful gift of healing. I believe we are all born with the ability to heal, but, over time the healing diamond within gets painted over with layers of stored emotions. The emotions are from events in our lives that we have not dealt with but shelved. To embark on a spiritual journey is to paint strip, to strip away and release all of the emotions, to drop the ego and find out who you are. Not the person you have become to please others but the real you that is deep within us all somewhere. So for me my life continues healing horses and training healers so that in time more and more horses can be heard. They have a voice if only we are prepared to listen.

I hope this book has made you think, what is my horse trying to tell me? How is he or she feeling? How can our relationship improve? What do I need to change to improve the relationship between me and my horse? If just one of you has voiced these questions then this book has done its job.

When I was on holiday on Bodmin November 2013, the day before I left I wanted to go for one last walk to find a wild herd of ponies. We walked across the moors until we found ourselves on top of a hill, there in front of us were a dozen ponies. A small herd, I stood and looked taking in the beautiful view. Some of them were quietly grazing, a couple snoozing and one in a thick hedge foraging and probably self medicating. I spoke to the ponies and they were happy for me to move close. I stood with them and felt how grounded they were and peaceful. There was no stress or anxiety, I wanted nothing from them and they were happy in my company.

I had been thinking about this last chapter and what to write and I asked them about it. I asked them "what did they want from us?" what came back was "for us to listen and be at one with horses, to be willing to learn horse from the horses. Not to dominate but form a partnership and work together."

I stood with the herd a while longer and then thanked them and quietly walked away, as I headed back down the hill I turned for one last glimpse of the peacefulness that surrounded the herd.

We eventually reached the car and driving back to our cottage I witnessed another scene entirely. It was late on a Sunday afternoon and over to our right we saw horses galloping. Then we realised we were witnessing a round up. There was a Landover with its horn blowing and two people on ponies with plastic sticks galloping behind the herd. We stopped and watched as they drove them off the moor and then followed them down the road. The young foals were clearly distressed and the mares were screaming for their young. After a while they were turned into a farmyard and as we drove past I saw the gate close behind them.

The following morning as we were driving off the moor we drove past the farm. There were mares cantering up and down the road screaming, looking at the mess on the road they had probably been doing this all night. As we drove past the farm I could see the young foals calling back from behind the locked gate. A tragic and cruel weaning, the ponies words from the day before were ringing in my ears. "Not to dominate but to work together........"

UNTIL THE NEXT TIME

For those interested in training with Elaine details can be found on www.equine-therapy.info

Made in the USA
Charleston, SC
06 November 2016